WITHDRAWN

Joseph Seamon Cotter, Jr.

COMPLETE POEMS

Joseph Seamon Cotter, Jr.

COMPLETE POEMS

Edited by James Robert Payne

The University of Georgia Press · *Athens and London*

© 1990 by the University of Georgia Press
Athens, Georgia 30602
All rights reserved

Designed by Mary Mendell   Set in Janson
The paper in this book meets the guidelines for permanence
and durability of the Committee on Production Guidelines
for Book Longevity of the Council on Library Resources.
Typeset by Tseng Information Systems, Inc.
Printed and bound by Thomson-Shore, Inc.

Printed in the United States of America

94 93 92 91 90   5 4 3 2 1

Library of Congress Cataloging in Publication Data
Cotter, Joseph Seamon, 1895–1919.
[Works. 1990]
Complete poems / Joseph Seamon Cotter, Jr.; edited by
James Robert Payne.
p. cm.
ISBN 0-8203-1152-9 (alk. paper). ISBN 0-8203-1181-2
(pbk.: alk. paper)
I. Payne, James Robert.   II. Title.
PS3505.O8623A125   1990
811'.52 – dc19   88-33073CIP

British Library Cataloging in Publication Data available

Frontispiece: Joseph Seamon Cotter, Jr. Reprinted
from Hammond, *In the Vanguard of a Race* (New York, 1922),
facing p. 168. Moorland-Spingarn Research Center, Howard
University.

FOR AVIS AND MARINA

Contents

Contents

Out of the Shadows:
An Unfinished Sonnet-Sequence

Poems

Contents

Preface

Joseph Seamon Cotter, Jr.: Complete Poems makes available for the first time reliable texts of all the poems of an important Afro-American poet of the years just preceding the 1920s Renaissance of black American literature. Texts of Cotter's poems have been established through collation of all extant texts of possible authority, including original manuscripts and typescripts housed at the Western Branch of the Louisville Free Public Library in Louisville, Kentucky. Included in this edition are seven previously uncollected poems which were discovered in manuscript or typescript among the Cotter family papers. Also included are another thirty-three poems that have been, with one exception, available until now only in hard-to-find early 1920s issues of the *A.M.E. Zion Quarterly Review*. Cotter's reputation as a gifted precursor of the 1920s Renaissance has been almost entirely based on the twenty-five poems of his *The Band of Gideon* collection, published in Boston in 1918. With this edition, the known and accessible canon of an important early modern black American poet is significantly enlarged.

In preparing the introductory essay as well as in establishing the texts of the poems, I have drawn extensively on Cotter's manuscripts and typescripts at the Western Branch of the Louisville Free Public Library. This important body of Afro-American literary and biographical materials, almost all previously unstudied, allows us to develop a much fuller picture than we have had before of Cotter's life and work. With the help of Carmen Samuels, librarian at the Western Branch Library, I was able to locate materials such as Cotter's boyhood school reports and documents pertaining to the tragic illness that took his life at the age of twenty-three. Throughout the

xi

papers there is evidence that Joseph Seamon Cotter, Sr., a well-known poet in his own right, recognized and nurtured his son's poetic talent. In addition to helping establish the poet's life, the manuscripts of Joseph Seamon Cotter, Jr., provide extensive documentation of the painstaking revision process through which Cotter obtained the subtle and varied patterns of sound and striking, often ironic, turns of phrase that characterize his poetry.

Cotter's literary manuscripts and typescripts are without question a highly significant Afro-American cultural resource. Comparable to significant manuscript collections at the Schomburg Center for Research in Black Culture in New York City and at the Moorland-Spingarn Research Center at Howard University, the Cotter manuscripts remain essentially unprocessed and are to be found at a neighborhood library that may fairly be said to be off the beaten track of even many veteran researchers. Most of the manuscripts are written on a porous type of notebook-filler or pad paper which is not long lasting. Now more than seventy years old, these papers are brittle; some are torn and beginning to flake. In order to provide a complete record of these important literary materials as well as access to them for scholars and students who may not be able to travel to Louisville, the Textual Commentary and Apparatus give full descriptive information on manuscripts and significant typescripts, including a record of manuscript alterations. These descriptions of the manuscripts along with the record of variant readings derived from all surviving poetic texts of possible authority give the reader all the data used in establishing the texts of Cotter's poems for this edition. Readers will find, too, that the Textual Commentary and Apparatus convey, sometimes indirectly, considerable information on Cotter's life and his habits and methods of composition.

My first thanks go to Trudier Harris and Thadious Davis of the University of North Carolina at Chapel Hill. Their invitation to me to write the "Joseph Seamon Cotter, Jr." article for their volume of the *Dictionary of Literary Biography, Afro-American Writers before the Harlem Renaissance* (Detroit: Gale, 1986), led to the research that ultimately resulted in this complete edition of the poems. Mary Yearwood of the Schomburg Center for Research in Black Culture in New York City alerted me to the scarce, early issues of the *A.M.E.*

Zion Quarterly Review containing Cotter's little known posthumous publications. I wish to convey my sincere thanks to Ms. Yearwood for this help and for her interest in the project. Carmen Samuels of the Western Branch of the Louisville Free Public Library helped and encouraged me daily as I studied the Cotter papers during three extended visits to Louisville. Her positive concern helped make this work a pleasure. Ann Allen Shockley, Special Collections, Fisk University Library, provided me with documentation of Cotter's time at Fisk. I wish to thank her for that help and also for her generous encouragement.

I am grateful to my wife and colleague Avis Kuwahara Payne whose collaboration with me in this work from the beginning and at every succeeding stage has made this a better book than it would have been otherwise. And many good ideas were contributed by my daughter, Marina.

I give warm thanks to colleagues who helped me solve specific problems related to this study, especially Richard Barksdale, University of Illinois at Urbana-Champaign; Fredson Bowers, University of Virginia; SallyAnn Ferguson, North Carolina A & T State University; Sara Hanna, New Mexico State University; Eugene Levy, Carnegie Mellon University; John Moffitt, New Mexico State University; Joseph Skerrett, University of Massachusetts at Amherst; and James Woodress, University of California at Davis. Special thanks go to Eugene Cunnar, New Mexico State University, who helped in many ways.

I received extensive assistance from staff members at a number of libraries, and I wish to thank in particular Esme E. Bhan, Manuscript Division, Moorland-Spingarn Research Center, Howard University; Julian Chesnutt, Archives, University of Louisville Library; W. Paul Coates, Manuscript Division, Moorland-Spingarn Research Center, Howard University; Caroline Davis, Manuscripts, Syracuse University Library; Jerry Ann Dimitrov, John Grant Crabbe Library, Eastern Kentucky University; Tom Owen, Archives, University of Louisville Library; Virginia Pearson, Kentucky Library, Western Kentucky University; Roger Steeb, New Mexico State University Library; and Emily Walhout, Houghton Library, Harvard University. Thanks are due also to members of the staffs of the archives or libraries of Atlanta University; Central State University, Wilberforce, Ohio; the Library of Congress; the Filson Club, Louisville; the University of Kentucky; the Louisville Free Public Library (main branch); the University of Oklahoma; the University of Texas at Austin; and Wilberforce University.

I give sincere thanks to Thomas Blue, Jr., and Lyman Johnson of Louisville for sharing their recollections of the Cotter family with me.

It is a pleasure to acknowledge support of a National Endowment for the Humanities Summer Stipend at the early stage of my research on Cotter and grant support from the New Mexico State University College of Arts and Sciences Research Center at later stages. A semester's sabbatical leave during the final stage of the project helped a great deal, and I am grateful for that support.

During the last phase of my work on this volume, two anonymous, specialist outside readers for the University of Georgia Press provided valuable encouragement and expert suggestions for my revision. I was fortunate, too, to have the expert assistance of University of Georgia Press editors Angela Ray and Nancy Grayson Holmes during the final stages of preparation of my manuscript for publication.

Malcolm Call, director of the University of Georgia Press, offered sensitive and very useful advice and counsel throughout this work. I thank him for that help and for his faith in this book.

Joseph Seamon Cotter, Jr.:

TOWARD A RECONSIDERATION

Joseph Seamon Cotter, Jr., was born September 2, 1895, in Louis-
ville, Kentucky, one of three children born to Maria F. Cotter, née
Cox, and Joseph Seamon Cotter, Sr. Both parents were members of
the Louisville educational community. Before her marriage, Maria
Cox served as teacher and principal, and the senior Cotter had a
distinguished career as teacher, principal, and poet. Joseph Cotter,
Sr., had been a precocious child who learned to read at the age of
three, benefitting from the stimulation of a mother who had the
gifts, according to her son, of "a poet, storyteller, a maker of plays."[1]

Because of family financial exigencies, the senior Cotter had to
leave school at the age of eight to work at a variety of jobs until
age twenty-two, when Dr. William T. Peyton, an important black
Louisville educator, discovered his poetic talent and encouraged
him to return to school. Joseph Seamon Cotter, Sr., went on to a
long and significant career as educator and poet, with many pub-
lications extending from *A Rhyming* (1895) to his *Collected Poems*
(1938) and beyond.[2] Cotter Sr. was principal of the Louisville school
named for his friend Paul Laurence Dunbar at the time of Cotter
Jr.'s birth, and by then the family was relatively well off and in their
own home at 2306 Magazine Street in Louisville. Propitiously, the
younger Cotter was born at home in the very room in which, on
Thanksgiving of the year before, Dunbar had read his poems at a
family party. As Joseph Seamon Cotter, Sr., later proudly recorded:
"Here for the first time in the South he [Dunbar] read the Negro
dialect poems that afterwards made him famous."[3] Although the

younger Cotter would completely eschew the dialect style that we see in much of Dunbar's and the senior Cotter's work, the circumstances of the young Cotter's birth were auspicious. The young man was born into a strong family tradition of poetry traceable at least to his father's mother and highlighted by his father's literary achievements and the family friendship with Dunbar, one of the most highly regarded poets of his day.

By all accounts, Joseph Seamon Cotter, Jr., enjoyed a normal boyhood, with no premonitory signs of future health problems. His boyhood home housed the good private library that his father had collected over the years. The home library was especially rich in poetry, and books of poetry were among the favorites of the young Joseph, who, with help from his older sister, Florence, became a precociously early reader just as his father had been. In his unpublished memoir entitled "Joseph S. Cotter, Jr.," Joseph Seamon Cotter, Sr., gives a glimpse of his son in the library: "When able he searched my large poetic library. Keats was his favori[t]e. He never tired of the 'Ode on a Grecian Urn.'"[4] Although the precise titles of the books in the Cotter family library are not known, if the whole body of the younger Cotter's poetry is any gauge, the family collection must have given the boy very early and fairly extensive access to varied strands of the classical European poetic tradition as well as additional access to Afro-American traditions beyond what he gained directly from the family. Certainly his own work would point to a writer immersed in both European and Afro-American traditions from an early age.

In his boyhood the younger Cotter was a good athlete and especially liked football, despite a rather slight physique. He performed the usual boyhood jobs of delivering newspapers and cutting grass. Abram Simpson, a friend in the neighborhood with whom Joseph worked at gardening, went on to become one of the youngest black American captains in the Great War and was a probable source of inspiration for Cotter's important war poetry. After completing primary grades at the Western School, the young Cotter went on to Louisville Central Colored High School where he pursued the very traditional curriculum of Latin, English, history, mathematics, and science. Joseph's report cards from the Western School and from

Central High are invariably signed by his high school principal father, and they definitely reflect the young man's intellectual propensities. The future poet earned especially high marks in Latin, English, history, and mathematics at Central High. Beyond his academic work the younger Cotter was noted for a very strong interest in world affairs including racial issues. In June 1911, at the age of fifteen, Joseph graduated from Central High School with second highest honors.[5]

Joseph was always exceptionally close to his older sister, Florence Olivia. According to their father, it was Florence who taught Joseph to read and write, and it was Joseph's intense grief over the death of his sister, the father wrote, "that discovered to him his poetic talent."[6] After his graduation from Central High, Joseph joined his sister at Fisk University in Nashville. Cotter is listed as a freshman in the Fisk University *Catalog* for 1911–12 and as a sophomore in the 1912–13 *Catalog*. Although documentation of Cotter's experience at Fisk is scarce, we know from the masthead of the *Fisk Herald* that he served on the staff of that monthly published by the "Literary Societies and Clubs of Fisk University."[7] Apart from his precociously early reading, Cotter's work on the *Fisk Herald* represents the first documented indication of his literary predilections.

During Cotter's second year at Fisk, Florence wrote home that her brother had contracted tuberculosis, and Joseph had to return to Louisville where he was put under the close supervision of the physician Dr. Siegel Frankel. For the remainder of his life the young Cotter fought the disease that was then a major killer of black Americans. Soon Florence, too, was home with tuberculosis, and within a year, on December 16, 1914, Cotter's sister, perhaps his closest friend, was dead.[8]

After his return home from Fisk, Cotter secured employment as an editor[9] and writer for the Louisville newspaper the *Leader* and worked as long as he could. Newspaper clippings preserved with the Cotter family papers in Louisville reveal that Cotter, in his early twenties, took responsibility as a spokesman for the interests of the black community. In an article from the *Leader* dated November 10, 1917, Cotter gave his personal reactions upon learning of a recent Supreme Court decision which helped to begin to limit "legal" discrimination in housing. The article is worth quoting briefly, for it gives a hint of the personality of the young man: "Reaching the High School campus, where our school children, two thousand strong, had gathered for a Community Sing, I heard definitely that the [Supreme Court] decision, banishing forever the legalized ghetto from our land, was a reality. My heart filled with a mighty joy. And as I stood listening to the childish treble of those Children of the Shadows, there came over me a strange calm, and I said to myself, 'This day is for them.' " [10] The figure "Children of the Shadows" in the quoted passage anticipates the working title, "Out of the Shadows," used on typescripts of what probably would have been Cotter's second book.[11] In other *Leader* articles Cotter revealed his interest in a range of subjects including the experience of black soldiers, the post–Great War world order, and the need for firmness by blacks in dealing with "those who actually hate us" as well as with " 'friends' who dispense patronizing advice about as freely as the good Lord gives air." [12] All in all, Cotter's newspaper writings reveal an extremely well-informed young man of often penetrating wit.

More important than the newspaper work, Cotter's poetic talent rapidly unfolded between the years 1915 and 1918. On June 26, 1918, the Cornhill Publishing Company in Boston published Cotter's book *The Band of Gideon and Other Lyrics*.[13] The collection contains the tribute "To Florence" [24],* which may have been Cotter's first poem,[14] and twenty-four more, among which are poems reflective of the young man's early strength with both traditional poetic modes and newer, experimental approaches. W. E. B. Du Bois thought highly enough of one of the seemingly more traditional *Band of Gideon* poems, "Sonnet to Negro Soldiers" [13], to feature it prominently in the June 1918 "Soldiers Number" of the NAACP journal the *Crisis*.[15] The modernist work in *The Band of Gideon*, including such poems as "A Prayer" [3], "Is It Because I Am Black?" [11], and "The Mulatto to His Critics" [2], clearly places Cotter among the important poetic innovators of the period. The introduction to *Gideon*, contributed by the poet Cale Young Rice, documents Cotter's contact with Rice, a Louisville resident who corresponded with Harriet Monroe and contributed to her *Poetry Magazine*, which

---

*Throughout this edition, references to poem numbers appear within brackets.

was a focal point of the modernist movement in poetry in the second decade of the twentieth century.[16]

Cotter did not rest with the publication of *The Band of Gideon* in the summer of 1918. Throughout the summer and into the fall Cotter worked on the "Out of the Shadows" love sonnet sequence [26–44] as well as on an eclectic group of poems [45–58], a number of which offer varied responses to a sense of impending death. Both the sonnet sequence and the eclectic group were intended to form sections of a second book, which never materialized because of Cotter's rapidly failing health. By January 1919 it was evidently necessary for the dying young man to dictate his work to his father.[17] And the end seemed to come as suddenly as Cotter's talent had emerged. The final section of Joseph Seamon Cotter, Sr.'s memoir "Joseph S. Cotter, Jr." is headed "His Passing" and gives the following brief account of the death of the young poet: "Monday morning February 3rd [1919], he realized that the end was near and seemed to brace himself for his last struggle. He made no complaint, but talked to all who happened in. He said to a young lady: 'Please excuse me if I fall asleep while you are talking.' About two hours after that he choked to death in my arms." [18]

It seems certain that it was Joseph Seamon Cotter, Sr., who, acting upon a recognition of his son's genius, attended to the posthumous publication of the sonnet sequence and the eclectic group of poems that the young poet worked on in the last months of his life.[19] In any case, in its third quarter issue for 1920 the *A.M.E. Zion Quarterly Review* carried Cotter's sonnets under the title "Out of the Shadows" [26–44], and a year later the same journal carried the final posthumous series, "Poems" [45–58], a collection which, like *The Band of Gideon*, reflects Cotter's interest in both traditional and experimental poetic style. Issues of the *Zion Quarterly Review* of the early 1920s have for some time been available mainly in specialized archives, and the journal may be overlooked by many scholars of American literature. For whatever reason or combination of reasons, published commentary on and general discussion of Joseph Seamon Cotter, Jr., over the last sixty or so years reflect no real familiarity with the two groups of Cotter's poems published in the *A.M.E. Zion Quarterly Review*.[20] In addition to the posthumously published poems, Cotter left among his papers drafts of a number of poems that are published for the first time in this edition as well as drafts of several plays.[21]

Cotter's sole book, *The Band of Gideon*, has not been overlooked as have the *Zion Quarterly Review* series of poems. In his pioneering anthology *The Book of American Negro Poetry*, judicious poet and critic of the 1920s Renaissance James Weldon Johnson observed of *The Band of Gideon*, "This is a volume of less than thirty pages, but it assays an uncommonly high percentage of genuine poetry." Readers familiar with Johnson's criticism will recognize this as high praise. In our time, poet and scholar Eugene B. Redmond judged Cotter "one of the most promising figures in Afro-American poetry" essentially on the basis of *Gideon*.[22] Yet in spite of such recognition, *The Band of Gideon* has never fully received the detailed critical response it clearly merits.

As shown in the Apparatus of this edition, the *Gideon* manuscripts reveal that Cotter experimented with more than one arrangement of the poems before the order of the published version was established. Thus, in one prepublication arrangement, "A Prayer" [3] is given as the opening poem of the collection. The title poem, in first position in the published text, was placed toward the center of the volume with poems of black consciousness.[23] Whatever merits the earlier, superseded arrangements of the *Gideon* poems may have possessed, the ordering of the poems as published suggests a thoughtfully structured work with identifiable beginning, middle, and final sections.

Though chosen by James Weldon Johnson for his highly selective *Book of American Negro Poetry* and appearing in a number of anthologies since Johnson's early black Renaissance collection, the significance and power of the title poem [1] of *The Band of Gideon* has not really been acknowledged in published commentary. In the five stanzas of "The Band of Gideon" Cotter boldly figures that Old Testament protector of the Israelites:

> The band of Gideon roam the sky,
>
> . . . .
>
> The thunder's roll is their trump's peal,
> And the lightning's flash their vengeful steel.

Cotter's effective use of detail and language from the King James translation of the book of Judges is seen most notably in the refrain: Gideon's people

cry aloud
With each strong deed,
"The sword of the Lord and Gideon." [24]

Some readers have viewed "Gideon" as essentially a simple, picturesque adaptation of traditional, rural southern sermon style. Thus, Robert T. Kerlin rather patronizingly asserts, "In it ["The Band of Gideon"] is re-incarnated, by a cultured, creative mind, the very spirit of the old plantation songs and sermons." [25] Yet just as we know how the traditional allegorical language of the sermons often encodes a sharply critical understanding of the contemporary scene, a reading of "The Band of Gideon" in relation to its time and provenance may suggest that Cotter chose to do more than simply memorialize an ancient people in, as Kerlin sees it, a "plantation" style poem.

Afro-American readers in 1918, at the close of World War I, would have been in an ideal position to appreciate Cotter's evocation of the righteous and militant Gideon. Following their military success against external enemies of their land, the biblical Gideon and his men had to face rejection from coreligionists who insultingly denied Gideon's normal request for cooperation and assistance upon his return from battle. [26] In 1918, in what was then called the Great War, black Americans fought successfully against external enemies of their land under the slogan "to make the world safe for democracy," only to face, like the biblical Gideon and his men, denial from many compatriots. [27] The final stanza of "The Band of Gideon," which recalls Gideon's righteous, punishing anger, in effect serves as a prophecy for what may come to the unjust of Cotter's own land.

There were particular, personal factors that may have prompted Cotter's interest in the Afro-American experience of the Great War. The war was in progress throughout his career as poet. Cotter's close boyhood friend, Abram Simpson, became one of the youngest black captains in the American army in World War I. With a longstanding interest in world affairs and with perhaps a particular interest in a special friend's army career in Europe, Cotter could follow developments of the conflict from Louisville and write newspaper articles about the war, though he could never hope to be a participant.[28] Yet his interest was such that in the course of a short career Cotter produced several poems that place him among the important poets of the war. In addition to the title poem, poems in *Gideon* that touch on war experience include "O, Little David, Play on Your Harp" [12] and "Sonnet to Negro Soldiers" [13]. With "Moloch" [51], a posthumously published poem, Cotter generates a strong response to war through the depiction of the true enemy of "lads of brown and black and white" as the pitiless ancient deity worshipped through the sacrifice of the young.

One of Cotter's most fully accomplished poems and the centerpiece of *The Band of Gideon*, "O, Little David, Play on Your Harp" [12] has received very little mention in published commentary on Cotter. It may be that "O, Little David" was ahead of its time with its unsparing presentation in 1918 of what seemed to Cotter a deeply rooted cruelty in human nature that is antecedent to war and a causal factor of such related phenomena as the pogroms in Russia and the atrocities against blacks in America and elsewhere. Paul Fussell has argued that the full genocidal horror of the Great War was beyond "any description . . . possible in the twenties or thirties."[29] Yet in 1918 in "O, Little David" Cotter struggled to articulate his understanding of the genocidal character of the motive behind the war and to link it to related events of his time in lines such as:

> A seething world is gone stark mad;
> And is drunk with the blood,
> Gorged with the flesh,
> Blinded with the ashes
> Of her millions of dead.

The formal structure of "O, Little David" clearly reinforces its theme of annihilation, with the catalog of contemporary horrors in the center section undercutting any pious hope which may seem to lie in the Judeo-Christian tradition evoked in the opening and closing refrain stanzas. The annihilating force in the modern world that Cotter identifies, the destructive fury that ravishes entire peoples, is personified in "O, Little David" as a Moloch-like figure, "A monster in the guise of man," a figure that recurs in Cotter's final war poem, "Moloch."

Although the white world of 1918 may not have been prepared for the picture Cotter offers in "O, Little David," important sections of Afro-America appear to have been more than ready for what Cotter does in the remainder of the center section of the poem, following the lines quoted above. A review of contemporary issues of the *New York Age*, the *Crisis*, and other important black periodicals of the time reveal that James Weldon Johnson, W. E. B. Du Bois, and other leaders insisted that atrocities against Afro-America, such as then recent lynchings and other appalling occurrences in East Saint Louis, Memphis, Waco, and other locations, be considered within a world context alongside and of at least comparable importance to atrocities committed by Germany and Russia against oppressed nationalities and political opponents.[30] In a few short lines of free verse in the middle of "O, Little David," the poem at the center of *Gideon*, Cotter places the crisis in America precisely parallel to the crisis of Armenian Christians ravaged by Turks, of Russian Jews subjected to Tsarist pogroms, and of the Belgians suffering under the Kaiser's occupation:

> Beneath the Crescent
> Lie a people maimed;
> Their only sin —
> That they worship God.
> On Russia's steppes
> Is a race in tears;
> Their one offense —
> That they would be themselves.
> On Flanders' plains
> Is a nation raped;
> A bleeding gift
> Of "Kultur's" conquering creed.
> And in every land
> Are black folk scourged;
> Their only crime —
> That they dare be men.

It is noteworthy how Cotter invests his reference to the experience of black America with the weight and power of the whole middle section of "O, Little David" by placing it in final position within the formulaic pattern "Their only," "Their one," "Their only."

The contrast between the experimental mode of "O, Little David" and the seemingly traditional form of "Sonnet to Negro Soldiers" [13],[31] which follows "O, Little David" in *Gideon*, reinforces our sense of Cotter's technical range and versatility. Probably the best known of Cotter's poems in his own day, "Negro Soldiers" was chosen for the special June 1918 issue of the *Crisis* honoring black Americans who served in World War I. This *Crisis* issue, which carried an unsigned editorial by W. E. B. Du Bois pointing up relationships between the fight for democracy in Europe and the fight for democracy in America, gave the sonnet a wide and often perceptive readership.[32]

As with Claude McKay's sonnets "To the White Fiends," "A Roman Holiday," and the famous "If We Must Die," which appeared in the *Liberator* in 1919, the year following the publication of "Sonnet to Negro Soldiers," the traditional form of Cotter's "Negro Soldiers" seems to hold up a principle of order in the face of the violence and chaos of war and strife in Europe and in America.[33] While Claude McKay's "If We Must Die" and his other militant postwar sonnets focus primarily on the struggle in America, McKay's 1919 sonnets and Cotter's 1918 "Sonnet to Negro Soldiers" do share an essential theme: Freedom, at home as well as in Europe, comes through taking action. Though employing language and figure derived from specific Great War experience, Cotter consistently associates the sacrifice of black soldiers in the European conflict with a more broadly based, more generally conceived action for freedom:

> They shall go down unto Life's Borderland,
>   Walk unafraid within that Living Hell,
>   Nor heed the driving rain of shot and shell
> That 'round them falls; but with uplifted hand
> Be one with mighty hosts, an arméd band
>   Against man's wrong to man . . . .

The famous "No Man's Land" between the Great War trenches is generalized to the "Living Hell" of "Life's Borderland." Black soldiers are to become "one with mighty hosts." Not until the final couplet does Cotter give the reader a glimpse of an actual enemy, that is, an enemy presented less abstractly than "man's wrong to man." And by now the reader may not be surprised that the essential enemy of the black World War I soldiers is not specifically Germans but prejudice. The action of black soldiers

> shall be a glorious sign,
> A glimmer of that resurrection morn,
> When age-long Faith crowned with a grace benign
> Shall rise and from their brows cast down the thorn
> Of prejudice. E'en though through blood it be.
> There breaks this day their dawn of Liberty.

When we consider that the enemy fought by Cotter's soldiers is first described broadly as "man's wrong to man" and then given more specifically as "prejudice," we may consider reading the last sentence of the sonnet as, at some level, prophetic of a changed post-war America as well as descriptive of Great War action in Europe. Such a reading would regard "Sonnet to Negro Soldiers" as a clear antecedent to McKay's militant 1919 sonnets and would correspond to the reading of "The Band of Gideon" offered above. In the editorial in the special *Crisis* issue that carried "Sonnet to Negro Soldiers," Du Bois predicted, "Out of this war will rise . . . an American Negro, with the right to vote and the right to work and the right to live without insult."[34] In a subtle fashion Cotter's "Sonnet to Negro Soldiers" seems to promise the positive outcome of Du Bois's prediction.

Although Cotter is unquestionably among the finest of the Afro-American poets of the Great War, he was of course by no means limited to war themes. Indeed, it could be argued that the most essential characteristic of Cotter's work is diversity of theme as well as technique. Following the title poem of *Gideon* are two unadorned free verse statements in conversational American idiom, "The Mulatto to His Critics" [2] and "A Prayer" [3], which unmistakably indicate Cotter's interest in experimenting with aspects of the newer American poetic style of the period. In "A Prayer," the third poem in *Gideon*, Cotter introduces a central motif of his work that he develops across the whole body of his writing, the desire for a poetic language adequate for consummation of longings that will not be fulfilled in actual life because of disability: "O God, give me words to make my dream-children live." Aspects of the dream of love, childbirth, and children, and the expressed desire for power to make present in language what will be absent in life recur throughout the principal series of Cotter's poems. This intertextual pattern, originating with the vision of "A Prayer," which was the first poem of "Gideon" in an early, prepublication arrangement of the collection, achieves its most focused and intense expression in the final sonnet [44] of the "Out of the Shadows" sequence, "It was a child that walked my dreams last night. / Smile of thy smile and eyes of thy dark eyes." The important woman and child figures of the sonnet sequence are discussed in detail in the section on the sonnets, below.

"The Mulatto to His Critics" [2], the second poem in *Gideon* as published,[35] is the first of an important group of thematically interrelated poems on aspects of black identity which also includes "And What Shall You Say?" [10] and "Is It Because I Am Black?" [11] as well as technically more traditional pieces like "Sonnet to Negro Soldiers" [13]. Recalling Walt Whitman in its rhythms and catalog style, "The Mulatto to His Critics" initially challenges those who would classify people by race:

> And of what race am I?
> I am many in one.
> Thru my veins there flows the blood
> Of Red Man, Black Man, Briton, Celt and Scot.

With line lengths governed by the sense of a sequence of statements rather than by a preordained metrical scheme, natural syntax without "poetic" inversion, and generally colloquial American diction, "The Mulatto to His Critics" reveals Cotter's genuine ease with important technical aspects of the newer poetic style of the era. His frequent use of reformed spelling, such as *thru* in "Mulatto" and elsewhere, signifies, it seems, the young man's intention to identify with modern trends. With its questioning of divisive racial classification, "The Mulatto to His Critics" recalls Walt Whitman's and later Charles Chesnutt's and others' premonitions of a new American people arising from a fusion of disparate peoples.[36] Yet at the end of the poem, Cotter goes beyond the theme of "many in one" to express a strong affirmation of black identity, with which he tellingly associates his poetic gift.

The challenging tone of the opening of "The Mulatto to His Critics" is amplified in Cotter's "And What Shall You Say?" and "Is It Because I Am Black?," both of which comprise penetrating interrogation of a projected white figure or stance by the black personae. The abrupt, uncompromising attitude of these poems clearly prefigures the post–World War I shift to a more militant or questioning stance in significant sectors of Afro-America, as signalled also by poetry of Claude McKay, Fenton Johnson, and others.[37] In his *Book of American Negro Poetry*, James Weldon Johnson astutely links Fenton Johnson's technical innovations with the new mood of Afro-America toward the end of the war: "in the war period he [Fenton Johnson] broke away from all traditions and ideas of Negro poetry, in both dialect and literary English. Moreover, he disregarded the accepted poetic forms, subjects, and language, adopted free verse, and in that formless form wrote poetry in which he voiced the disillusionment and bitterness of feeling the Negro race was then experiencing."[38] Much of what James Weldon Johnson states here in regard to Fenton Johnson applies as well to modernist work of Cotter represented by poems like "And What Shall You Say?" and "Is It Because I Am Black?" In these poems of Cotter as in work of Fenton Johnson described by James Weldon Johnson, both dialect and artificial "literary" English are avoided in favor of natural idiom. Free verse displaces conventional metrical and stanzaic patterns as the poets dispense with traditional poetic themes in order to directly present contemporary attitudes of the post-war era. The "disillusionment and bitterness" that James Weldon Johnson saw in Fenton Johnson's poems such as "Tired" and "The Scarlet Woman" do not come to the surface in Cotter's poetry, at least not to the degree that we see in Fenton Johnson.[39] Nevertheless, the energetic, experimental style and sharply challenging tone of poems like "And What Shall You Say?" and "Is It Because I Am Black?" clearly justify James Weldon Johnson's view of Cotter as a highly significant proto-Renaissance figure: "[Cotter's] best work places him in the post-war class of Negro poets and ranks him high among them. These later poems reveal a sensitive imagination and delicate workmanship; at the same time, their texture is firm. 'And What Shall You Say?' was a much-quoted poem immediately following the war." [40]

The Band of Gideon concludes with two poems expressive of intensely personal feeling, "To Florence" [24], a tribute to the sister who fostered Cotter's growth in literature and to whom the *Gideon* collection was dedicated,[41] and "Compensation" [25], a testimony to the cost and pain involved in the creative process. "Compensation" reveals Cotter's interest in "medieval" motifs, which he of course shared with other modern poets and which we see again in the "Out of the Shadows" sonnet sequence [26–44]. Especially noteworthy is the way the final stanza of "Compensation" serves not only as the conclusion of the poem, but also as the conclusion to the book, recalling the traditional envoi found at the end of medieval and Renaissance poetry collections.

The poems of *The Band of Gideon* have been generally available since their publication by the Cornhill Company in 1918.[42] With the exception of "Rain Music" [52],[43] the remainder of Cotter's poetry, work beyond *Gideon*, which taken together comprises over half the body of his work, has been essentially unavailable to most readers, hidden in early 1920s issues of the *A. M. E. Zion Quarterly Review* or unpublished.

The nineteen sonnets [26–44] published in the third quarter 1920 issue of the *Zion Quarterly* under the title "Out of the Shadows: An Unfinished Sonnet-Sequence" were evidently composed in the late summer and fall of 1918, the final autumn of the young poet's life.[44] Working in the strict English or Shakespearean sonnet form maintained throughout the sequence, Cotter experimented with and discarded two versions of a first sonnet to the series[45] before the final version [26], which, unlike the two rejected trial versions [64, 65], focuses directly and passionately on the body and soul of the beloved. Throughout the whole of the sonnet sequence, the speaker explores incidents of love with great particularity. Thus, in the opening lines of Sonnet II [27] the time before love is recalled:

> but a child I lightly held thee then,
> Nor cared to wake the starlight in thy eyes,
> Nor dreamed this glad unrest.

In Sonnet III [28] the speaker explores very specifically the reciprocal relationship between an "old love" and the new. Although the extraordinary particularity with which the speaker deals with incidents of the beloved may lead readers to assume the sonnet sequence is addressed to an actual woman, with documentation presently available it is not possible to establish this point with certainty. The figure of the woman of the sonnets may refer to an actual person or may be a projected figure of imagination.

In Sonnet V [30] the focus shifts from the woman to the male speaker, who alludes to his precarious situation:

> Here where men, weeping, spend a passing day,
>   See one grand sun-set and its after-glow,
> Feel a brief passion, then the heart's decay,
>   God rest me as I stand beneath the blow.

If we read these sonnets as expressive in some degree of the poet's particular situation, we may feel a special poignancy in the quoted lines. Manuscript evidence suggests that the lines were composed in the second week of September 1918, a time when Cotter's tuberculosis was very advanced.[46] He would succumb to the disease within five months. Yet there are suggestions of a kind of solace. The dying young man may have seen his predicament as ultimately one with that of all mankind: "There is no rest where weary mortals dwell." What is more important, there is the possibility of love, as expressed in the closing couplet of the fifth sonnet. That love — passionate, erotic, familial, or devoted to God — can definitely bring peace is a central motif recurring throughout the whole body of Cotter's work. At the end of the fifth sonnet Cotter acknowledges that after the experience of love more pain will come. The paradox of the seemingly reciprocal relationship between love and pain fascinated Cotter and is addressed in "Is This the Price of Love?" [5], "Remembrance" [22], and other poems of the *Gideon* collection as well as in the sonnet sequence.

The exploration of connections between desire and pain is strikingly enlarged in Sonnet VI [31]:

> These are the little things that stir the heart,
>   Awaken memories of the yester-years,

> Arouse old sorrows with a painful dart,
> Becloud the brow and flood the eyes with tears.

The strong evocation of the body of the beloved that follows these lines and which recurs throughout the sonnets is generated in part by an onrushing, impossible-to-contain awareness on the part of the speaker of the rapid failing of his own body: "All must I give for fate is merciless / And garbs my youth in age's sable gown." The speaker acknowledges he must renounce "all but the vision" of the beloved, and concludes the sixth sonnet with an unforgettably strong couplet: "Though wreathed in tears and deep in sorrow laid, / I have the vision and it shall not fade."

As we move toward the center of the sonnet sequence, we see Cotter endeavoring to place his highly personal "vision" within a very wide, virtually cosmic context in which the speaker removes his love from the limitations of ordinary time and place to associate it with the passion of creation:

> When this gay earth whelmed with a mad desire
>   Swung out of chaos in a nebulous form,
> God borned a passion tinged with heavenly fire
>   And wreathed about with many an ancient charm.
> Garbed in the beauty of the vaulted skies,
>   To primal calm the passion burned its way,
> When man was young and earth was Eden-wise,
>   And life the music of a golden day.
>
>   (Sonnet VIII [33], 1–8)

The figuring here of creation and of primordial passion may recall Milton's *Paradise Lost*, especially sections of Books VII and VIII of that seventeenth-century epic that Cotter doubtless read in his father's library. Yet specific literary or possibly oral sources for the elaborate, metaphysical conceit extending through Sonnets VIII [33] and IX [34] that melds the theme of erotic love with that of God's love expressed in original creation are not really known with certainty. Some readers may hear the echo and influence at the center of the sonnet sequence of an American rhetorical tradition which very boldly uses and adapts biblical accounts of creation, a mode seen long ago, for example, in the verse "Preface" of Edward Taylor's "Gods Determinations" (1682) and much later, after Cotter, in James Weldon Johnson's "The Creation" in *God's Trombones* (1927).[47] Perhaps elements of services at the Episcopal Church of Our Merciful Saviour in Louisville, where Cotter was baptized on February 16, 1908,[48] were drawn upon for the imagery of divine creation antecedent to human passion.

Though direct introduction of the figure of a child as fulfillment of the love celebrated throughout the sonnet sequence does not occur until Sonnet XIX [44], the child figure is anticipated in language of the opening lines of Sonnet XVI [41]:

> God knows the burdened soul's dark sorrowing
>   When hearts are sadly pregnant with old fears.
> God knows the labour that it is to bring
>   The child of laughter from the womb of tears.

Through the metaphorical use of such words as "pregnant," "labour," "child," and "womb," Cotter introduces thoughts of childbirth. He also, especially in the third and fourth lines quoted above, utilizes the figure of childbirth to allude to his own painful difficulties as creator, as poet.

The speaker in Sonnets VIII [33] and IX [34] projects an elaborate conceit which links his passion back to its ultimate antecedent, the love of God revealed in creation. Fusion of themes of human passion and divine love is seen again, most remarkably, in the figuration of the mother and child in the nineteenth and final sonnet [44]:

> It was a child that walked my dreams last night.
>   Smile of thy smile and eyes of thy dark eyes
> Gave to his raptured face the gleaming light
>   Of that lone star which hung in Bethlehem's skies.

The dream child, associated with the Christ Child, the light of whose "raptured face" recalls the light of the star "in Bethlehem's skies," gives a vision of fulfillment of human passion as well as hope of rebirth and renewal as promised in Christianity. Early in *Gideon*, in "A Prayer" [3], Cotter's speaker describes his incapacitation and prays,

As I lie in bed,
Flat on my back;
There passes across my ceiling
An endless panorama of things —

. . . .

Women in the holy glow of motherhood,

. . . .

O God, give me words to make my dream-children live.

The full figuration of the child, mother-beloved, and lover that we find in the concluding sonnet may be read as the fulfillment of the free verse "Prayer" in *Gideon* for language adequate for the consummation of desires that will not be achieved in actual life because of disability and premature death. Yet at the very end of the nineteenth sonnet [44] Cotter strikes a decidedly jarring, dissonant chord, referring to the desired offspring with his beloved as the child "That never was, nor is, nor e'er shall be."[49] Rather than ultimately finding redemptive consolation and solace in literary art, Cotter exquisitely figures forth his beloved and child of the sonnets to lovingly, with the utmost care, measure out what will never be attained.

If Cotter had lived to complete his second book, it almost certainly would have included the nineteen love sonnets followed by a seemingly diverse group of poems [45–58] which were published after the poet's death in the *Zion Quarterly*'s "Poetic Section" (second quarter, 1921) under a general title of "Poems." Although these "Poems" may be approached productively in a number of ways, it is worth noting how this final group may be expressive of varied responses to a sense of impending death. On one hand, poems such as "I Shall Not Die" [48], "To ———" [50], "Why?" [54], "Sonnet" [55], and "Love's Demesne" [56] reflect a sense of personal or individual finitude. On the other hand, in "A Woman at Her Husband's Grave" [46], "Moloch" [51], and "Theodore Roosevelt" [58], death is treated in relation to the other, beyond self. Finally, such poems as "Rain Music" [52] and "Africa" [57] may be read as offering a ground for hope in the face of individual mortality.

The speaker of "Love's Demesne" evokes memory to develop a contrast between a present time of sorrow and former times of "sorrow never born." The contrast of a recollected time of happiness with a bleak present was drawn somewhat more sharply in the earliest manuscript draft of "Love's Demesne," in which the last lines of the second stanza are: "My thoughts sweep o'er remembered scenes / To this drear morn." Although we know that on at least one occasion an editor suggested to Cotter that he ameliorate harshness of theme,[50] the deletion of "drear" in line 8, beginning with the second manuscript of "Love's Demesne," doubtless derives from Cotter's tendency to revise to enhance sound patterns. The tone and patterns of sound of "Love's Demesne," particularly the short, two stress lines that end each stanza, may evoke for the reader tonal effects obtained by Emily Dickinson, whose poetry was being discovered in Cotter's day. In "Love's Demesne" the treatment of memory, especially recollection of the interrelated pleasure and pain of love, recalls a central theme of the sonnet sequence.

If "Love's Demesne" reminds the reader of the dilemma of the poet on the plane of time, time past through memory flooding into present time, "Why?" [54] is suggestive of the finitude of the body. As in "Love's Demesne," in "Why?" Cotter's method is the representation of contrast to establish difference and meaning. The figure of the physically vital, beautiful child, "Her olive face and curly hair / Are tidings of earth-peace," juxtaposed to the speaker's reference to "my wasted form," will recall to some readers the sharply drawn contrast of the bodies of the beloved woman and child with the "form . . . / So wasted, frail . . ." of the speaker in the sestet of Sonnet XIX [44]. "Why?" displays Cotter's ability to deftly place and utilize a familiar phrase. Consider how the placement of the common expression "But what am I to her?" in the last line works to undercut sharply the cheery surface mood established in the lines that precede.

The eleventh of the final group of fourteen posthumously published poems, entitled simply "Sonnet" [55], gives probably the strongest expression of personal grief of any of Cotter's published writings. Only in the brief, unpublished poem beginning "Full well he knew the gall of broken spirit" [61] does Cotter move closer to direct expression of despair. Interestingly, although Cotter adopted the English or Shakespearean sonnet form for the "Out of the Shadows" sequence, he chose the perhaps more challenging Italian or Petrarchan form for this individual sonnet of the final series.[51] Did extremity of grief evoke strict self-discipline in choice of poetic form? Although formally contrasting with the free verse "And What Shall You Say?" [10], in its first stanza "Sonnet" reveals an approach similar to that of the earlier poem from *The Band of Gideon*. Both "Sonnet" and "And What Shall You Say?" project powerful questions, an approach Cotter adopted in a number of his most successful poems, including "Is It Because I Am Black?" [11], "Is This the Price of Love?" [5], and others. The octave of the sonnet under discussion offers questions of an afflicted young man desirous of retaining religious faith. The speaker asks "if the Mighty God / Cares aught about the little deeds of men" and asks why lives may be circumscribed by seemingly arbitrary fate:

> Does He who lightly holds th' eternal rod,
>> Now taut, now loose, the threads of Why and When,
>> Give passing heed . . . .

In the classic Italian sonnet a problem or situation is presented in the octave which is resolved or commented on in the sestet. As we have seen, the opening stanza of "Sonnet," which disarmingly begins "I sometimes wonder," poses some of the most difficult questions of human life. Adopting a Job-like stance in the second stanza, the speaker offers no easy answers but voices a steadfast hope, "yea surely, God must care." Yet undercutting the note of resolution that the sonnet structure conventionally calls for in the sestet is the bleak, death-foreshadowing imagery which pervades the whole poem: "hungry sod," "one-time flesh but now the wind-blown clod," "[t]orn, broken sheaves," "ghostly reapers."

Among a second group of the posthumous "Poems," including "A Woman at Her Husband's Grave" [46], "Moloch" [51], and "Theodore Roosevelt" [58], death remains central, but the subject is the death of persons other than the writer himself. The young Cotter is not alone in mortality. "Moloch" memorializes America's Great War soldiers, "lads of brown and black and white," who like Cotter must die in youth. According to Cotter Sr.'s note at the bottom of typescripts of "Theodore Roosevelt," [52] the young poet's final poem was this sonnet on the death of the President who died just three weeks before Cotter's own death. Cotter Jr.'s political orientation tended to be very close to that of W. E. B. Du Bois as revealed in *Crisis* editorials of the day, and it is worth comparing the attitude toward Roosevelt expressed in Cotter's sonnet with that expressed in the lead *Crisis* editorial in the issue that appeared just after the President's death:

> We have lost a friend . . . . Even in our hot bitterness over the Brownsville affair we knew that he *believed* he was right . . . . [I]n 1917 he justified our trust when at the time of the East St. Louis riots he alone, of all Americans prating of liberty and democracy, uttered his courageous pronouncement at the meeting in Carnegie Hall.
>
> "Justice with me," he shouted, "is not a mere form of words!"[53]

Within the historical context suggested by this *Crisis* editorial, Cotter Jr.'s treatment of Roosevelt in the final poem does not seem idiosyncratic. The poem itself marks the parting of an idealized senior male figure, and perhaps at some level it registers the young Cotter's knowledge that soon there would be a final parting with another, closer, older male figure, his father. In any case, the poet's father was almost certainly more intimately involved in the process of the composition of "Theodore Roosevelt" than he was with any other of his son's poems. Cotter dictated the sonnet to his father, and the father's note at the end of the typescripts of the sonnet conveys a special intimacy and sense of parting, "The above sonnet was young Cotter's last poem. He dictated it to his father."[54] Of all of Cotter's poems, "Theodore Roosevelt" is the only one that was published with such an annotation regarding its provenance.

The post–World War I issue of the *Crisis* which carried the tribute to Theodore Roosevelt was essentially devoted to Africa, with articles exploring the depredations of European imperialism, the more independent role Africa was expected to assume in the postwar period, and the importance of Afro-American involvement in what Du Bois termed the "redemption of Africa."[55] Featured is a letter by Du Bois from France which alludes to his planning for a Pan-African Conference to meet in Paris during the Peace Conference at Versailles in order to advise the Peace Conference on African issues.[56] I point to this *Crisis* issue as an indicator of the new, postwar feeling for Africa of which Cotter's penultimate poem of the

"Poems" group is clearly a part. The speaker of "Africa" [57] asserts the continent's honorable history and her coming resurgence to "her ancient place." In her fight for freedom Africa will redeem and validate the "boasting creeds" of nations that only talk of freedom:

> She stands where Universal Freedom bleeds,
> And slays in holy wrath to save the word
> Of nations and their puny, boasting creeds.

With its impressive articulation of righteous anger and the necessity to couple words of freedom with action for freedom, "Africa" bears comparison with Cotter's better known poems from *Gideon*, "The Band of Gideon" [1] and "Sonnet to Negro Soldiers" [13]. On a personal level, it may be that during the composition of "Africa" the opportunity to identify imaginatively with ideas of renewal and rebirth gave the young poet hope in the face of individual mortality.

The Band of Gideon
and Other Lyrics

[1]   *The Band of Gideon*

The band of Gideon roam the sky,
The howling wind is their war-cry,
The thunder's roll is their trump's peal,
And the lightning's flash their vengeful steel.
  Each black cloud
  Is a fiery steed.
  And they cry aloud
  With each strong deed,
"The sword of the Lord and Gideon."

And men below rear temples high
And mock their God with reasons why,
And live in arrogance, sin and shame,
And rape their souls for the world's good name.
  Each black cloud
  Is a fiery steed.
  And they cry aloud
  With each strong deed,
"The sword of the Lord and Gideon."

The band of Gideon roam the sky
And view the earth with baleful eye,
In holy wrath they scourge the land
With earth-quake, storm and burning brand.
  Each black cloud
  Is a fiery steed.
  And they cry aloud
  With each strong deed,
"The sword of the Lord and Gideon."

The lightnings flash and the thunders roll,
And "Lord have mercy on my soul,"
Cry men as they fall on the stricken sod,
In agony searching for their God.

Each black cloud
Is a fiery steed.
And they cry aloud
With each strong deed,
"The sword of the Lord and Gideon."

And men repent and then forget
That heavenly wrath they ever met,
The band of Gideon yet will come
And strike their tongues of blasphemy dumb.
Each black cloud
Is a fiery steed.
And they cry aloud
With each strong deed,
"The sword of the Lord and Gideon."

[2]   *The Mulatto to His Critics*

Ashamed of my race?
And of what race am I?
I am many in one.
Thru my veins there flows the blood
Of Red Man, Black Man, Briton, Celt and Scot,
In warring clash and tumultuous riot.
I welcome all,
But love the blood of the kindly race
That swarthes my skin, crinkles my hair,
And puts sweet music into my soul.

[3] *A Prayer*

As I lie in bed,
Flat on my back;
There passes across my ceiling
An endless panorama of things —
Quick steps of gay-voiced children,
Adolescence in its wondering silences,
Maid and man on moonlit summer's eve,
Women in the holy glow of motherhood,
Old men gazing silently thru the twilight
Into the beyond.
O God, give me words to make my dream-children live.

[4] *The Deserter*

I know not why or whence he came
  Or how he chanced to go;
I only know he brought me love,
  And going — left me woe.

I do not ask that he turn back
  Nor seek where he may rove,
For where woe rules can never be
  The dwelling place of love.

For love went out the door of hope
  And on and on has fled,
Caring no more to dwell within
  The house where faith is dead.

or whence

I know not why he came
Or how he changed to go;
I only know he but me love,
And going—left me woe,

I do not ask that he turn back
~~Nor seek where he may~~
~~The faith over which he strove,~~
For places love rules can never be
The dwelling place of love,

~~For love is life and love is light~~
For love went out the door of hope
And on and on has fled,
Caring no more to dwell within
The house where faith is dead.

Joseph S. Cotter Jr.

Holograph manuscript of "The Deserter" [4, MS]. Western Branch, Louisville Free Public Library.

[5] *Is This the Price of Love?*

Never again the sight of her?
    Never her winsome smile
Shall light the path of my journeying
    O'er many a weary mile?
Never again shall her soft voice come
    To cheer me all the while?
O Thou, who hearest from above,
Tell me, is this the price of love?

Never again the touch of her lips?
    Never her dark, brown eyes
Shall shine on me with the dancing joy
    Of stars in the summer skies?
Never again shall my song be aught
    Save minor chords of sighs?
O Thou, who hearest from above,
Tell me, is this the price of love?

[6] *Ego*

Day passeth day in sunshine or shadow,
 Night unto night each cycle is told;
Sun, moon and stars in whirling and glamour,
 All unto all the creation unfold.

What of the strivings, what of the gropings,
 Out from the darkness into the light?
What of the weepings, what of the grievings
 Now from the day to a passionless night?

Stars of the stars, heavens of the heavens,
 Rising or falling or pausing a span,
Each to the great "I am" replying
 E'en as the crystal, even as man.

Chant of the worlds from aeon to aeon,
 Song of the soul from dust unto dust,
Dream of the clods that, upward and starward,
 Rise to the call of the primal "Thou must."

Space beyond space, eternity's vision,
 Chaos to chaos, calm unto calm,
World beneath world, heaven above heaven,
 Life but the urge, death but the balm.

[7] *Dreams*

There is naught in the pathless reach
    Of the pale, blue sky above,
There is naught that the stars tell, each to each,
    As over the heavens they rove;
That I have not felt or have not seen
Clad in dull earth or fancy's sheen.

There is naught, in the still, mauve twilight
    When the dreams come flitting by,
From lands afar of eternal night,
    Or lands of the sunswept sky,
For countless spirits within me dwell
With heaven's effulgence or dark hell.

[8] *Then I Would Love You*

Were you to come,
With your clear, gray eyes
As calmly placid as, in summer's heat,
At noontide lie the sultry skies;
With your dark, brown hair
As smoothly quiet as the leaves
When stirs no cooling breath of air;
And shorn of smile, your full, red lips
Prest firmly close as the chaliced bud,
Before the nectar-quaffing bee ere sips;
I would not know you.
I would not love you.

But should you come,
With your love-bright eyes
Dancing gaily as, on summer's eve,
The stars adown the Western skies;
With your hair, wind-caught
And circled round your shining face
In fashion which no hand ere wrought;
And your full, red lips poised saucily,
As the slender moon midst an hundred stars,
And held aloof in daring taunt to me,
Then I would know you,
Then I would love you.

[9] *I'm A-waiting and A-watching*

I'm a-waiting and a-watching for the day that has no end,
For the sun that's ever shining, for its rays that ever blend;
For the light that casts no shadows, for the sky that's ever fair,
For the rose that's ever blooming as its fragrance fills the air.

I'm a-waiting and a-watching for the land that knows no night;
Where the terrors of the darkness are dispelled in morning's light,
Where the murmurs of the breezes blend themselves into a song,
And the silvery carol echoes to the heavens, soft and long.

I'm a-waiting and a-watching for the song that's never o'er,
For the joy that's never ending on that light-emblazoned shore,
For the peace that shall enfold me with the heavens' holy breath,
For the glory that shall greet me, for the life that knows no death.

Brother, come!
And let us go unto our God.
And when we stand before Him
I shall say—
"Lord, I do not hate,
I am hated.
I scourge no one,
I am scourged.
I covet no lands,
My lands are coveted.
I mock no peoples,
My people are mocked."
And brother, what shall you say?

[11] *Is It Because I Am Black?*

Why do men smile when I speak,
And call my speech
The whimperings of a babe
That cries but knows not what it wants?
Is it because I am black?

Why do men sneer when I arise
And stand in their councils,
And look them eye to eye,
And speak their tongue?
Is it because I am black?

O, Little David, play on your harp,
That ivory harp with the golden strings
And sing as you did in Jewry Land,
Of the Prince of Peace and the God of Love
And the Coming Christ Immanuel.
O, Little David, play on your harp.

A seething world is gone stark mad;
And is drunk with the blood,
Gorged with the flesh,
Blinded with the ashes
Of her millions of dead.
From out it all and over all
There stands, years old and fully grown,
A monster in the guise of man.
He is of war and not of war;
Born in peace,
Nurtured in arrogant pride and greed,
World-creature is he and native to no land.
And war itself is merciful
When measured by his deeds.
Beneath the Crescent
Lie a people maimed;
Their only sin —
That they worship God.
On Russia's steppes
Is a race in tears;
Their one offense —
That they would be themselves.
On Flanders' plains
Is a nation raped;
A bleeding gift
Of "Kultur's" conquering creed.
And in every land
Are black folk scourged;

Their only crime —
That they dare be men.

O, Little David, play on your harp,
That ivory harp with the golden strings;
And psalm anew your songs of Peace,
Of the soothing calm of a Brotherly Love,
And the saving grace of a Mighty God.
O, Little David, play on your harp.

They shall go down unto Life's Borderland,
    Walk unafraid within that Living Hell,
    Nor heed the driving rain of shot and shell
That 'round them falls; but with uplifted hand
Be one with mighty hosts, an arméd band
    Against man's wrong to man — for such full well
    They know. And from their trembling lips shall swell
A song of hope the world can understand.
All this to them shall be a glorious sign,
    A glimmer of that resurrection morn,
When age-long Faith crowned with a grace benign
    Shall rise and from their brows cast down the thorn
Of prejudice. E'en though through blood it be,
There breaks this day their dawn of Liberty.

And Thou art One — One with th' eternal hills,
And with the flaming stars, and with the moon,
Translucent, cold. The sentinel of noon
That clothes the sky in robes of light and fills
The earth with warmth, the flowering fields, the rills,
The waving trees, the south wind's elfin rune,
Are One with Thee. All nature is in tune
With Thee, O Father, God — and if one wills
To humbly walk the fragrant, leaf-strewn path
And kneel in reverence 'neath the vaulted sky,
Hearing the hymnals of the waving trees
And prayers of the soughing winds — what hath
He less of heaven in him than we, who cry,
"God in our creeds doth dwell and not in these?"

[15] *Sonnet*

I would not tarry if I could be gone
  Adown the path where calls my eager mind.
  That fate which knows naught but to grip and bind
Holds me within its grasp, a helpless pawn,
And checks my steps when I would travel on.
  Forever shall my body lag behind,
  And in this Valley with the Moaning Wind
Must I abide with never a glimpse of dawn?

Though bends my body towards the yawning sod,
  I can endure the pain, the sorrows rife,
That hold me fast beneath their chastening rod,
  If from this turmoil and this endless strife,
Comes there a light to lead Man nearer God,
  And guide his footsteps toward the Larger Life.

[16] *Memories*

The burnished glow of the old-gold moon
  Shines brightly over me.
A thousand stars, like a thousand isles
  In a dark and placid sea,
Bring memories of a golden night,
  Bedecked in Autumn's hue
And fragrant with the lilac's bloom,
  That brought me joy—and you.

[17] *Love*

Love is the soothing voice of gods
   To which men ever list.
Love is the ease of soul's travail
   And sorrow's alchemist.

Blue eyes, gray eyes,
 All the eyes that be,
Hold within their changing depths
 Wealth of charm to me.

Dark-eyed maid, of moment's fancy,
 Gay as stars above;
Is it you that I adore,
 Or is it Love I love?

[19] *An April Day*

On such a day as this I think,
    On such a day as this,
When earth and sky and nature's whole
    Are clad in April's bliss;
And balmy zephyrs gently waft
    Upon your cheek a kiss;
Sufficient is it just to live
    On such a day as this.

[20] *Supplication*

I am so tired and weary,
  So tired of the endless fight,
So weary of waiting the dawn
  And finding endless night.

That I ask but rest and quiet —
  Rest for days that are gone,
And quiet for the little space
  That I must journey on.

I have found joy,
  Surcease from sorrow,
From qualms for today
  And fears for tomorrow.

I have found love,
  Sifted of pain,
Of life's harsh goading
  And worldly disdain.

I have found peace,
  Still-borne from grief,
From soul's bitter mocking
  And heart's unbelief.

Now may I rest,
  Soul-glad and free,
For Lord, in the travail,
  I have found Thee.

Forget?
Ah, never!
Your eyes, your voice, your lips.
Those little ways of love,
Half-childish yet all-wise
That held me but a slave to you,
Will never loose their bonds.
The power to forget
Would Fate but yield to me.

Remember?
Ah, too well!
The hurt, the pain, the grief.
The wrack of nightly dreams,
The ruth of brooding days,
Have left a lesion in my soul
That only Heaven can heal.
Remembrance is the lot
That Fate does hold for me.

Old November, sere and brown,
Clothes the country, haunts the town,
Sheds its cloak of withered leaves,
Brings its sighing, soughing breeze.
Prophet of the dying year,
Builder of its funeral bier,
Bring your message here to men;
Sound it forth that they may ken
What of Life and what of Death
Linger on your frosty breath.
Let men know to you are given
Days of thanks to God in heaven;
Thanks for things which we deem best,
Thanks, O God, for all the rest
That have taught us — (trouble, strife,
Bring thru Death a larger Life) —
Death of our base self and fear —
(Even as the dying year,
Though through cold and frost, shall bring
Forth a new and glorious spring) —
Shall shed over us the sway
Of a new and brighter day,
With Hope, Faith and Love alway.

Sister, when at the grassy mound I stand
Which holds in cold embrace thy mortal frame,
The tears unbidden rush into my eyes
And wash away from me all save the sight
Of thy pure life and patient suffering.
And ever and anon comes memory
Of days gone by when health's bright sun did shine
Upon us both. And tho within the Cloud
I stand, content I am to think of thee
And live as best I may, till by thy side
In God's own time, I lay me down to rest.

[25] *Compensation*

I plucked a rose from out a bower fair,
    That overhung my garden seat;
And wondered I if, e'er before, bloomed there
    A rose so sweet.

Enwrapt in beauty I scarce felt the thorn
    That pricked me as I pulled the bud;
Till I beheld the rose, that summer morn,
    Stained with my blood.

I sang a song that thrilled the evening air
    With beauty somewhat kin to love,
And all men knew that lyric song so rare
    Came from above.

And men rejoiced to hear the golden strain;
    But no man knew the price I paid,
Nor cared that out of my soul's deathless pain
    The song was made.

Out of the Shadows:
An Unfinished Sonnet-Sequence

[26] *I*

The starlight crowns thee when thou standest there,
   The shadows clothe thee in their robes of gray,
The night-winds sighing thru thy dusky hair
   Echo the music of a vibrant day.
Such is the glory and the sight of thee
   That filled my eyes this happy hour gone by,
Such is the glamour and the light of thee,
   The lasting burden of love's ancient cry.
And that I love thee so I shall be singing,
   (Dark are thy eyes and golden is thy smile),
Carols of joy to distant heavens ringing,
   (Pure is thy soul and free thy heart from guile).
Hear as I sing, O Sweet, my lover's part,
Tender thy smile and tender be thy heart.

Had I but known when first I saw thee there,
    Slender of form and happy in thy smile,
Would I have oped my hungry heart to bear
    The burden now it carries all the while?
For but a child I lightly held thee then,
    Nor cared to wake the starlight in thy eyes,
Nor dreamed this glad unrest. O where and when
    Did love first spring from out the bourne of sighs?
Was it the touch of thy soft hand, the chords
    Of love were wakened by, or thy warm breath
O'er gladsome smile or tender-spoken words,
    That crowned my heart with this soul-passioned wreath,
And bade me then to know thee for my own —
Thou dark-eyed child unto a woman grown?

"What of the old love?" cries my heart to me;
  Ah let it die, I say; ah let it die.
Burdened it was with love's satiety,
  Weep for it, heart, and give it sigh for sigh.
Keep but its purity to give the new,
  Shed all the dross its sorrowed years had borne;
Keep but its joy to cheer the journey thru,
  Dry all the tears that cloud my new love's morn.
Give me the passion that the old love brought,
  Add to the measure of my new love's fire;
Give me the laughter that the old love wrought,
  Add to the wealth of my new love's desire.
What is the old but treasure for the new,
Found in love's bounty of the good and true?

Why should I sing when every living voice
    Carols in joy for my love's holiday?
Why should I laugh when all the skies rejoice,
    Blue-girt and silvered in each sun-kissed ray?
Yea, though the skies, the earth, each God-sent thing,
    In flowering field, or glen, or deep-set moor,
Croon softly each to each, still shall I sing,
    Tho weak the chords or be the accents poor.
These shall I bring for my love's golden fare,
    These shall I give as down my days she trips —
Song-burthened zephyrs for her wind-blown hair,
    Garlands of laughter for her crimson lips,
Laughter or song, 'tis but love's joyous fee,
Deep from the treasure of my heart to thee.

There is no rest where weary mortals dwell,
    There is no peace where sorrow bides the time,
Save in love's boundless arms, where rise and swell
    Life's fairest moments into hours sublime.
Here where men, weeping, spend a passing day,
    See one grand sun-set and its after-glow,
Feel a brief passion, then the heart's decay,
    God rest me as I stand beneath the blow.
Send to my heart a purging flame of love,
    Suaging my tears with its consuming fire,
Whelm me with passion that shall never rove
    Save to the beckon of my love's desire.
For love I crave tho follows grief amain —
A fleeting moment from an hour of pain.

These are the little things that stir the heart,
   Awaken memories of the yester-years,
Arouse old sorrows with a painful dart,
   Becloud the brow and flood the eyes with tears,
Soft, soothing hands that weave love's ancient charm,
   And softer voice that croons love's roundelay,
Firm, rounded breasts that crown thy slender form,
   Dark, wistful eyes deep with the joy of day.
All but the vision of thy loveliness
   That dwells within my heart and will not down,
All must I give for fate is merciless
   And garbs my youth in age's sable gown.
Though wreathed in tears and deep in sorrow laid,
I have the vision and it shall not fade.

When you sit there the shadows come and go
    In merry gambol 'round your shining face,
And press their purpled shades about the glow
    Of crimson on your cheeks. In happy grace
They kiss your lips as night enfolds the skies,
    And peacefully they come and softly dwell
Deep in the caverns of your darkling eyes,
    Casting the witchery of their magic spell.
O then, I know God made my hungry heart
    For you to rule by word or glance or smile.
'Tis all of earth and heaven's better part
    To live within the thrall your lips beguile.
Nor need I gaze at stars for in your eyes
There gleams the starlight of a thousand skies.

When this gay earth whelmed with a mad desire
 Swung out of chaos in a nebulous form,
God borned a passion tinged with heavenly fire
 And wreathed about with many an ancient charm.
Garbed in the beauty of the vaulted skies,
 To primal calm the passion burned its way,
When man was young and earth was Eden-wise,
 And life the music of a golden day.
Down from the ages over hungered souls
 And love-lorn hearts its flaming breath is spread,
Searing with crimson life's eternal scrolls,
 Warming the spirit when the flesh is dead.
Crowned with the years the passion comes to me,
Clad in the glory that is one with thee.

Passion of fire that sears my hungry heart
  Deep with the image of thy shining face,
Clothe me in dreams that breathe the magic part
  Of olden wraiths and many a by-gone grace!
Hard to the realms of dim, forgotten days,
  When first I lived and spent my numbered years,
Spirit of mine trips down the garland ways
  To love-born moments void of earthly fears.
In sportive joust I stood thy pledgéd knight,
  Keeping the faith with my victorious arms,
Or when there gleamed the crimson battle light
  Thy heart of love made easeful war's alarms.
Old days are gone, but love renews each age,
Letters of gold on God's eternal page.

Purpled to softness comes the twilight hour,
  Out of the travail of the feverish day,
Soothing the hot, quickened breath with the power
  Of Gilead's balm to ease the sinner's way.
Girt with the memories of a kindred time,
  Pensive I sit beneath the summer sky,
Dreaming of love that fires my feeble rhyme,
  Longing for words to clothe the old-time cry.
Passion that wings me to forgotten years,
  Give to my heart this flame of mad desire,
Send to my dreams from out the anguished tears
  Words that shall breathe of an immortal fire!
O, but to sing an unforgetting chord —
Better it is than wield the conqueror's sword.

Silent I love thee. When thou deignst to speak
  I love thee more. When happily thou smilest,
Beloved, then upon the soul's high peak
  I stand, deep in the spell which thou beguilest.
Bourne of the shadows, thy soft wind-blown hair
  Prisons my heart within the joy thou bringest.
Dusk is a-quiver, all vibrant the air,
  When with thy darkling eyes gaily thou singest.
Silent the song and yet there falls the strain,
  Far o'er the thrall wherein my heart thou holdest;
Captive I be, but neither bar nor chain,
  Nor power save love about my heart thou moldest,
Silence or word or smile or dark eyes gleaming —
Morsels of heavenly fare, joys of my dreaming.

Gray veils of dusk bestrewed with purple threads
  Hold earth, a-fevered, in their soothing power.
Soft coronals of twilight round our heads,
  Silent we sit and dream this holy hour.
Night-winds are stirring thru the stately pines,
  Shrouded in shadows 'gainst the star-lit sky;
Night-birds are singing in the fragrant vines,
  Soft to their mates an eery lover's cry.
'Tis then I see thee most, and seeing love thee,
  Knowing the dusk but beauty's trailing gown;
'Tis then I feel and know the stars above thee,
  Jewels to garnish my love's golden crown.
Why should I long for garish light of day,
When twilight visions crowd my happy way?

O love, my love, thou 'rt in the passing crowd,
  But none shall see thee save the eyes that burn;
O love, my love, thou singest long and loud,
  But none shall hear thee save the ears that yearn.
O love, my love, thou 'rt in the solitude
  Of foam-crest oceans and the tangled wood,
But none shall know thee in thy changing mood,
  Save minds deep-nurtured in the heart's dark flood.
O love, my love, thou 'rt in the blue-girt sky,
  And bound in murmurs of the sighing breeze,
But none shall feel thy lilting melody,
  Save hearts that quaff thy spirits-passioned lees.
O love, thou wert a beggar shouldst thou hold
Thy blood-warm spirit to hearts bitter cold.

Life is a dream in the Eternal Sleep,
  And love the fancy of its little hour.
How like a vision, when there slowly creep
  Known faces and unknown that peer and lower
O'er hidden corners, and of sorrow's pall
  Make hideous mockery; where alternate
Hope and despair, mad agony and all
  The aching pangs of ruth bow to dumb Fate,
The prescient power that dims their moment's light.
  O may love's passionate and pulsing breath
Fire fancy's bourgeouny 'round my dark night
  And crown my sleep with heaven's star-gold wreath.
Life without love, it were a tear-swept moan,
Heaven denied, mid depths of hell unknown.

Beyond the lifted clouds the dark sweeps by,
  The stars grow dim in more abundant light,
The paling moon shines faintly down the sky,
  And journeys slowly with the ghost of night.
The sun, still hidden like a frightened fawn,
  Sheds virgin gleams about the golden feast
Of nature at the freshing fount of dawn —
  There is a new day browsing in the east.
O were the dawn a happy herald's song
  Of love that capers to the beck of Youth!
O were the day a gladdened chord among
  These hollow echoes of a naked truth!
And shall Love never from her largess spare
Dawn's breath of glory for a moment's fare?

God knows the burdened soul's dark sorrowing
 When hearts are sadly pregnant with old fears.
God knows the labour that it is to bring
 The child of laughter from the womb of tears.
And oh, life's tempered joy, cold, bitter band,
 Sorrow embowered in bright pleasure's wreath,
Heart's passion, quickened by love's fiery breath,
 Heart's hope, denied by fate's despoiling hand;
The golden vision of God's shining face
 Mid halting steps and body's shambling dress —
All this the travail and the bitterness,
 The gall that sours the spirit's wonted grace.
And must the body bear the blood-writ scroll
To wake the murmurs of th' immortal soul?

It is not life's bright hope or hell's dark terrors,
  Or earthly benison for my poor heart,
Or spirit prescient of the mind's dumb errors
  That bid me shun the easy, bloodless part.
Nor is it that my eyes shall soon forget
  The flaming breath of sunset in the west,
Or that my lips in frigid firmness set
  Shall soon be careless of thy lips at best.
Dark are the dim, remembered paths of earth
  Where once our feet in laughing measures sped,
Dark are the days that echo my heart's dearth
  As I stand halting 'mongst the living dead.
I should not quail at heaven's beckoning moan,
Only that going I shall leave thee lone.

[43] *XVIII*

Remembered is your every trick of speech,
  Your lilting smiles to merry laughter grown,
The pregnant glances of your eyes, and each
  Soft, soothing touch my brow and hair have known.
And all your moods from joy to darkened sorrow,
  And all the dreams of which you are the whole,
And all the gleaming plans of life's tomorrow
  Have etched their deepening lines within my soul.
And there a figure limned in joy and grief
  Holds balm to Hope that treks hand in our hand,
Eternal symbol of our heart's belief,
  Hallowed by heaven's song and God's command.
Fate never dreamed the burdened heart could find
The splendored joy of love in faith enshrined.

Holograph draft of Sonnet XIX [44, MS¹]. Western Branch, Louisville
Free Public Library.

It was a child that walked my dreams last night.
Smile of thy smile and eyes of thy dark eyes
Gave to his raptured face the gleaming light
Of that lone star which hung in Bethlehem's skies
His slender hands played softly on my face
And lo! it was the touch I knew so well;
He spoke, and there I heard the tender grace
Of thy clear voice. And then the passioned swell
Of love that ~~draws~~ my pulsing heart to thine
Bade me to reach and take him to my side —
I saw thy beauty, but this form of mine,
So wasted, frail — and then I broke and cried.
God heard the cry and took the child from me,
That never was, nor is, nor e'er shall be.

Holograph manuscript of Sonnet XIX [44, MS²]. Western Branch, Louisville Free Public Library.

It was a child that walked my dreams last night.
　Smile of thy smile and eyes of thy dark eyes
Gave to his raptured face the gleaming light
　Of that lone star which hung in Bethlehem's skies.
His slender hands played softly on my face
　And lo! it was the touch I know so well;
He spoke, and there I heard the tender grace
　Of thy clear voice. And then the passioned swell
Of love that draws my pulsing heart to thine
　Bade me to reach and take him to my side —
I saw thy beauty, but this form of mine,
　So wasted, frail — and then I broke and cried.
God heard the cry and took the child from me,
That never was, nor is, nor e'er shall be.

Poems

[45] *Immortality*

From your life's blood to coin a trenchant word —
The past, the present and the future's ken
To hold — and weave it to a ringing chord
That sounds within the changing hearts of men.

Peace to his ashes!
I cannot for the soul of me
Sorrowing bow,
Tho I search thru the heart of me
Grieve for him now.
'Tis well he is gone
And heart-break is over,
A husband he was
But never a lover.

[47] *Night Winds*

The slender moon in its silvery sheen,
The golden stars with the blue between
Of a dreamy, summer sky;
And still the night winds sigh.

With the silvery moon to whisper to,
And the golden stars to kiss, mid the blue
Of a listening, summer sky,
For what should the night winds sigh?

[48] *I Shall Not Die*

Never shall I die
  While this untrammeled spirit-mine
  Shall in hope's constellation shine
And faith-embraced my soul shall lie.

O why are there eyes like these,
That sparkle and dapple and tease,
So wide with the morning, so deep with the night,
Dancing and gleaming in passioned delight?
O why are there eyes like these?

O why are there lips like these,
Caressed by the southern breeze,
That beckon and call and hold a slave
All who therewith each soul-cry lave?
O why are there lips like these?

O why are there arms like these,
That crumple and crush as they please
A weak man's heart, and in their embrace
Bring a glow of red to a strong man's face?
O why are there arms like these?

[50] *To* ———

Sunless days and starless nights,
    Bearing fruits of wrack and pain,
Purge my lips of lover's vows,
    Bid me never hope again.

Yet the longing of my soul,
    Oft denied, still faintly cries,
For the heaven of your smile,
    And the starlight of your eyes.

Old Moloch walks the way tonight
    On Flanders' poppied field,
Where foe meets foe in steel and might
    And never one shall yield.

Old Moloch of the fiery shrine,
    Deep in the throes of pain,
Cries for the bleeding anodyne
    Of flesh of youths again.

Heart of my heart went out tonight,
    Where Moloch holds the way,
To lads of brown and black and white
    Who blazon Freedom's day.

Tear down the shrine of Moloch there,
    From crimson field and glen,
Tear down the shrine of Moloch where
    It shames the hearts of men.

Holograph draft of "Moloch" [51, MS¹]. Western Branch,
Louisville Free Public Library.

On the dusty earth-drum
    Beats the falling rain;
Now a whispered murmur,
    Now a louder strain.

Slender, silvery drumsticks,
    On an ancient drum,
Beat the mellow music
    Bidding life to come.

Chords of earth awakened,
    Notes of greening spring,
Rise and fall triumphant
    Over every thing.

Slender, silvery drumsticks
    Beat the long tatoo —
God the Great Musician
    Calling life anew.

[53] *Reward*

Out of the silence
   I come to you,
Bringing a love
   Free as the dew.

I come and sing
   A heart's great love,
And passion of soul
   Pure as a dove.

But this I crave
   As you pass by—
A smile on your lips,
   A light in your eye.

[54] *Why?*

The little child across the street—
    Why does she wave to me?
What sees she in my wasted form
    To hail so joyously?

Her olive face and curly hair
    Are tidings of earth-peace,
Her golden smile's a wealth of joy
    That bids my sorrows cease.

To me she is a fairy sprite—
    A heavenly harbinger
Whose sun-kissed eyes are songs of God—
    But what am I to her?

[55] *Sonnet*

I sometimes wonder if the Mighty God
   Cares aught about the little deeds of men;
   And if their day and time can reach His ken
Or raise their breath beyond the hungry sod.
Does He who lightly holds th' eternal rod,
   Now taut, now loose, the threads of Why and When,
   Give passing heed — or be they one or ten —
To one-time flesh but now the wind-blown clod?

If men can die who never yet knew life,
   And, smiling, hold it is no strange affair;
Or live when death were welcome boon of strife,
   Torn, broken sheaves the ghostly reapers spare;
The saints must grieve for earthly sorrows rife,
   And God must heed, yea surely, God must care.

Old memories come trooping down
   The vistas of the years;
In blue-girt robes of pleasure clad
   Or garbed in tears.

Down from the days when hope was young
   And sorrow never born,
My thoughts sweep o'er remembered scenes
   Unto this morn.

Though motley company they are
   Of smile or tear or frown,
They hold aloft the burnished gold
   Of my heart's crown.

For through it all and over all
   There gleams the light serene,
On purpled walls and crimson heights
   In love's demesne.

A thousand years of darkness in her face,
   She turns at last from out the centuries' blight
   Of labored moan and dull oppression's might,
To slowly mount the rugged path and trace
Her measured step unto her ancient place.
   And upward, ever upward towards the light
   She strains, seeing afar the day when right
Shall rule the world and justice leaven the race.

Now bare her swarthy arm and firm her sword,
   She stands where Universal Freedom bleeds,
And slays in holy wrath to save the word
   Of nations and their puny, boasting creeds.
Sear with the truth, O God, each doubting heart,
Of mankind's need and Afric's gloried part.

Now with the dust that bore him he is one,
　　Silent, into earth's silent maw ye laid him.
Dimmed is his light, as with the setting sun,
　　He folds his steps unto the God who made him.
When shall the weak stand and rejoice again
　　To see his banner in the battle's light?
When shall the humble hear his voice again
　　Raised from the mountain of majestic right?
O ye shall see that banner gleam again
　　High o'er the ramparts of a nation's goal;
O ye shall hear that voice redeem again
　　The blood-stained conscience of a nation's soul.
Rise ye that tremble 'mid such fearful moan,
He stands anointed at Jehovah's throne.

Uncollected Poems

Whither bound and how goeth?
On what tempestuous sea
Hast thou deployed thy bark?
In what manner bloweth
Those winds that drive thee
On thy perilous way?
In what steel dost thou array
Thyself and be armed for the fray?
What pilot, enshrouded in the dark,
Dost guide thee
From the quay?

Democracy speaks

Bound I am for that endless shore,
Where dwelleth eternal liberty
Free from the tyranny
Of the benighted fetish of "Right Divine,"
Where dwelleth the verity
Of man's brotherhood to man,
Where standeth the open door
Thru which doth shine
The everlasting light,
That thru the darkest night
May yet be seen God's plan.

I launch my bark on the troubled sea
Of tyranny;
Flecked with the bloody foam
Of its martyred dead;
Strewn with the flesh of those who bled
That freedom yet may reign
O'er land and home.
Tossed by heresy,
By plotting foe and blundering friend,

My strength may wane
As light midst approaching dark,
But ever upright is my bark,
Ever forward is her prow
Till reached the destined end.
Armed with Godly Faith and Brotherly Love,
Piloted by Him who dwelleth above
I shall be then — where now
I sight the strand —
On freedom's holy land.

[60] *On Hearing Helen Hagan Play*

It seemed to me a little rivulet
That gently flows along its course,
By woodland and thru field,
And then its scanty bosom filled by rain,
A larger stream becomes
And flows till rocky crags and steppes are reached
And tossed by storms and lashed by winds
A raging cataract it is.
Spent its fury, now at last
In depths of placid lake,
Its voice once more is calm.

And thus your music moved me, thrilled me;
Gently first, in paeans of joy
It swept into my soul.
And then it rose, crescendo on crescendo
Until this very heart of mine
Did surge and strain as anchored ship in storm;
Tossed and billowed and at length o'er flowed
In soothing flood of harmony,
And softly then it spread o'er all
In blessed wealth of soul,
Its benediction sweet.

Full well he knew the gall of broken spirit,
The dream of life abundant turned a cross
To ever stand on failure's Golgotha;
Mute symbol of his crucifixioned soul.

Never, never shall I clothe
   All my foolish Fears in words.
Earth would weary with the song,
   Sorrows echo to the chords.

I shall bury Fear so deep
   It shall never dare to grope
From the shadows, save 'tis led
   By the standard-bearer Hope.

Your hands in my hands,
Happily meet;
Your eyes and my eyes,
Joyously greet;
Your cheek 'gainst my cheek,
Passingly sweet;
Your lips to my lips,
Rapture complete.

My lyre is strung with golden threads of love,
Harped to the tune of my heart's sorrowing,
My caroling from cloistered realms above,
Full-burthened with my spirit's borrowing
Of heavenly passion and its purity,
Of earthly longing and its hungered soul.
All, all my Sweet the song is but for thee,
In cadenced chord or organed swell and roll;
Its measured rythm but to hail thy grace,
Aery and free as ever summer skies;
Clearly its note unto thy shining face,
Thy soft, warm breath and wistful, darkling eyes.
Hear as I sing, O Sweet, my lover's part
Tender thy smile and tender be thy heart.

Down from the golden strings of my heart's lyre
  Fall lyric chords that sing a wondrous love.
Keyed to the melody of passioned fire,
  My flaming spirit wings the skies above
In eager search of heaven's harmony,
  To wake such kindred echoes in thy soul
As from a goddess to her devotee,
  In cadenced chord or organed swell and roll,
My song is raised unto the aery grace
  That light enfolds thee as the summer skies,
Clearly its note unto thy shining face,
  Thy soft, warm breath and wistful, darkling eyes.
Hear as I sing, O Sweet, my lover's part,
Tender thy smile and tender be thy heart.

Textual Commentary

The manuscripts of the poetry of Joseph Seamon Cotter, Jr., are with the Cotter family papers, housed in a small room containing the special Afro-American holdings of the Western Branch of the Louisville Free Public Library. Along with the literary manuscripts of the younger Cotter, the Cotter family papers include literary manuscripts of Joseph Seamon Cotter, Sr., records of the senior Cotter's activities as a prominent Louisville educator, family photographs, newspaper clippings, scrapbook materials, and various other family memorabilia.

Manuscripts

The literary manuscripts of Joseph Seamon Cotter, Jr., may be described in several distinct categories. First, there remain for many of his poems holograph drafts and fair handwritten copies, generally on separate pieces of tablet or pad paper but sometimes on the backs of letters or envelopes or other pieces of paper that the poet had at hand. These drafts and fair copies were written in pencil and often bear Cotter's signature or initials and a date. When both earlier and later manuscripts of a particular poem have survived, we find that Cotter tended to assign the date of the earliest manuscript draft to his subsequent manuscript copies. The surviving manuscripts on the blue-ruled, school or legal tablet paper that Cotter generally favored are now yellowish-brown with age, brittle, and often torn. Specific descriptive details that do not yield to generalization regarding these separate manuscript sheets are given in the notes on texts of individual poems in the Apparatus that follows.

In addition to the separate, pencil-written manuscript sheets described above, the remnant of a loose-leaf, ring-binder notebook of manuscripts and a relatively intact school tablet of poems written on ruled sheets comprise important parts of the Joseph Seamon Cotter, Jr., papers. For purposes of brief reference I have designated these two sets of manuscripts the ring-binder group and the school-tablet group. The ring-binder manuscripts are in what remains of a two-ring binder, written in pencil on both sides of ten leaves of blue-ruled white paper (236.5 × 188 mm, 25 mm head space), watermarked UTILITY LEDGER. The ring-binder pages bear a red vertical margin line set 26 mm from the edge of the sheet to the left on the front side of the leaves and to the right on the back side. There are two holes punched in the margins, one 37 mm from the top and the other 41 mm from the bottom, to accommodate the metal binder rings. At some time, all of the ring-binder leaves were pulled loose from the rings, as all the punched holes are torn through to the edge of the paper. The leaves were subsequently laid back in the remnant of the binder. When I studied Cotter's ring-binder manuscripts in July 1986, nine manuscript leaves were followed by fifty-one blank unruled white leaves; the tenth manuscript leaf was tipped in following the blank leaves. As described in the notes on texts of individual poems in the Apparatus that follows, several of the ring-binder manuscript leaves bear a penciled number in the upper left corner on the front side. Though the significance of these numbers is not fully clear, they may represent a system of pagination that was for some reason left incomplete. It is possible that the order of the ring-binder leaves has been changed and that some have been lost since the original compilation of the notebook by the young Cotter.

The notation "Property | of | Joseph S. Cotter, Jr. | Miscellaneous | Verse | By | Joseph S. Cotter, Jr." is inscribed in large cursive script on the outside of the heavy gray paperboard cover (approximately 235 × 195 mm) of the ring-binder notebook. This inscription appears to be in the hand of Cotter Jr. The inside of the cover bears two names printed by hand in faded purple or indigo ink: "Joseph S. Cotter" printed vertically above "Aime M. Taylor." The lower name may be "Alma M. Taylor." In any case, the reading is not certain. These names have been crossed out in what appears to be pencil. Following each name, in the same faded ink, are what seem to be initials. Very difficult to decipher, a mark somewhat resembling an "f" followed by, perhaps, an "h" appears after the name "Cotter". What appears to be an "f" followed by a faint comma and then an apparent "m" are written after "Taylor". The significance of these initials is unclear. The word "eight" is written in cursive script in the lower right corner of the inside of the notebook cover, and there are a number of ink blots, two or three of which are heart shaped, though whether by intention or not is hard to say. The word "eight" and the blots are in faded purple or indigo ink. The provenance of all of the inscriptions on the inside of the notebook cover is uncertain. At present, only the one cover and two somewhat triangularly shaped metal rings of the binder itself remain.

The ring-binder manuscripts provide fair, holograph texts of eight of the twenty-five poems published in *The Band of Gideon* (in order of appearance in the manuscript set: "Remembrance" [22], "The Mulatto to His Critics" [2], "The Goal" [21], "Then I Would Love You" [8], "Is It Because I Am Black?" [11], "And What Shall You Say?" [10], "Is This the Price of Love?" [5], "A Prayer" [3]), twelve of the fourteen poems posthumously published in the spring 1921 issue of the *A.M.E. Zion Quarterly Review* (in order of appearance in the manuscript set: "Reward" [53], "Why?" [54], "Immortality" [45], "A Woman at Her Husband's Grave" [46], "Looking at a Portrait" [49], "Night Winds" [47], "To ———" [50], "Sonnet" [55], "Love's Demesne" [56], "Moloch" [51], "Rain Music" [52], "Africa" [57]), and one poem, "On Hearing Helen Hagan Play" [60], published for the first time in the present edition. Ring-binder manuscripts of poems which appear in *The Band of Gideon* bear the abbreviation "Pub." usually penciled near the title. This abbreviation is in what appears to be Cotter Jr.'s hand and seems to mark poems published in *Gideon* in contrast with the other principal group of ring-binder poems which are marked "Copy" in pencil or, in one case, "Copy this.", again in what appears to be the young Cotter's hand. All the ring-binder poems marked "Copy" or "Copy this." are included in typescripts which seem to have been made in preparation for what would have been Cotter's second book. They were all eventually published under the heading "Poems" in the spring 1921 issue of the *Zion Quarterly Review*. Cotter's notations

"Copy" or "Copy this." were probably instructions to a typist, perhaps the senior Cotter, who prepared typescripts of the poems for publication. It is interesting to note that the one ring-binder poem which has never been published until now, "On Hearing Helen Hagan Play" [60], is the only poem of the group of manuscripts marked neither "Pub." nor "Copy". Additional descriptive details of the ring-binder manuscripts, including a record of manuscripts marked "Pub." or "Copy", may be found in the notes to texts of individual poems in the Apparatus.

While the ring-binder manuscripts provide holograph texts for sixteen poems of the eclectic groups published in *The Band of Gideon* and in the spring 1921 issue of the *Zion Quarterly*, the school-tablet manuscript group gives fair, holograph texts of Sonnets II–XV, XVII–XVIII of the nineteen-sonnet sequence [26–44] published in the late summer 1920 issue of the *Zion Quarterly* as "Out of the Shadows: An Unfinished Sonnet-Sequence," as well as the only known text, published for the first time in this edition, of a rejected trial opening sonnet [65] for the sequence.

The school-tablet manuscripts may be found in a relatively intact pad of now yellowish-brown, blue-ruled paper (247.5 mm to perforation, 14.5 mm perforation to binding × 204 mm; 26 mm head space to perforation on front side, 26 mm tail space to perforation on back side). The heavy white paper front cover of the school tablet is printed entirely in black and bears a large, lithographically reproduced drawing of the courthouse in Louisville. "Pencil Tablet | No. 3" is printed in the lower right corner of the illustration. Beneath the illustration "THE LOUISVILLE | SCHOOL TABLET" appears in large capital letters. This tablet cover is signed "J. S. Cotter Jr" in the lower left corner. The gray paperboard back cover bears the same signature, vertically inscribed in large script.

Sixteen leaves remain in the school tablet, and slight remnants suggest that numerous leaves have been removed both preceding and following those remaining. The "Out of the Shadows" sonnet sequence texts are written in pencil, one to a page, on both sides of the first eight remaining leaves of the tablet and on the front side only of the ninth leaf. The first manuscript leaf of the school tablet was detached at some time and laid back in; the other manuscript leaves were still attached to the red adhesive binding of the tablet when I studied it in July 1986. Particular details regarding individual school-tablet manuscripts are given in notes to texts of individual poems in the Apparatus.

Typescripts

In addition to the manuscripts surveyed above, an important body of typescripts of the poetry of Joseph Seamon Cotter, Jr., is housed with the Cotter family papers at the Western Branch of the Louisville Free Public Library. As with the holograph manuscripts, I will survey the typescripts and their significance in a general way here and describe unique aspects of individual typescripts in the Apparatus.

A group of eight typescripts on relatively small pieces of paper, doubtless cut from standard sized typing paper, may point to efforts by Cotter to achieve publication of his poetry in periodicals. These poems on "slips," the term I have used for brief reference, are typed one to a page on only one side. They were typed on a wine-colored ribbon with a typewriter apparently unique among those used to produce the Cotter Jr. manuscripts. The group includes copies of "And What Shall You Say?" [10], "A Prayer" [3], "To Florence" [24], "Is It Because I Am Black?" [11], "Then I Would Love You" [8], "Remembrance" [22], "The Mulatto to His Critics" [2], and "The Goal" [21], listed in order as found clipped together at the Western Branch Library. These slips are often signed by the poet in black ink and often bear his home address.

One of these typescripts, that of "Is It Because I Am Black?" [11, TS¹], carries notations which tend to confirm the thought that the slips were prepared for submission to periodicals. Clearly suggestive of editorial review, at the head of the "Is It Because" typescript in question is the note "Return │ J. F."; and in the lower left corner, another note appears: "not enough │ point — write some │ more stanzas offering │ contrast to first │ two — in spite of │ being black — │ Ed." Cotter may have used this early typescript as a submission to the NAACP monthly, the *Crisis*. The initials "J. F." may be those of Jessie Fauset, who we know began "working with W. E. B. Du Bois and the *Crisis*" in 1918, the year Cotter would have sent out "Is It Because I Am Black?" for consideration.[1] Though not provable with total certainty, the handwriting of the editorial notation on the "Is It Because" typescript resembles that of Fauset as exemplified on her manuscript materials preserved at the Schomburg Center in New York. Whether or not, in fact, Fauset did reject "Is It Because I Am Black?" for publication in the *Crisis*, it might be recalled at this point that Cotter's important "Sonnet to Negro Soldiers" [13] was accepted and prominently featured in the June 1918 "Soldiers Number" of the NAACP journal. All of the poems typed on the slips of paper were included in *The Band of Gideon* collection.

Clipped with the set of Cotter's poems typed on slips of paper is a black carbon typescript of his uncollected poem "Ode to Democracy" [59, TS¹] which bears a revealing handwritten annotation:

> This was 13th poem in Original
> "Band of Gideon"
> By Joseph S. Cotter, Jr.

This notation, apparently in the hand of Cotter Sr., alludes to a pre-publication version of *The Band of Gideon* still extant in the form of typescripts housed at the Western Branch of the Louisville Free Public Library. For purposes of brief reference I have designated these materials comprising the "Original 'Band of Gideon'" as the early "Gideon" typescripts. Cotter evidently prepared at least three copies of the early "Gideon" typescripts: A surviving cover sheet bears the notation "3 copies." (with "copies" underlined) in what appears to be the young poet's hand. Pages 1–11 and 14–20 of the original copy as well as one or two of the carbons of each of these pages survive (see Apparatus notes on texts of individual poems for listing of extant carbons). Original ribbon copies of pages 12–13 are lost, though a good carbon of the twelfth page has survived and provides the copy-text of "November" [23] for this edition. The black carbon copy of "Ode to Democracy" is styled like the early "Gideon" typescripts, evidently typed on the same typewriter, and probably represents page 13, though this cannot be proven, because the section of the "Ode" typescript where the page number would be has been cut away. Thus, the annotation on the "Ode" typescript may well suggest that it appeared on page 13 of early "Gideon." As may be seen on the listing of the early "Gideon" poems below, the thirteenth poem of that original arrangement was actually "Sonnet to Negro Soldiers" [13], appearing on typescript with page number 10. The order of poems of the early "Gideon" compilation is given below because Cotter was interested in intertextual relationships of his poems and evidently considered their ordering a matter of critical importance. Readers may be interested in comparing this early arrangement of the early "Gideon" poems with the order of poems as published in *The Band of Gideon* (1918) and as followed in the present edition. Numbers on the left represent the page numbers of the early "Gideon" typescripts. Note that on several of the typescript pages more than one poem appears.

p. 1   "A Prayer" [3]
           "The Mulatto to His Critics" [2]
p. 2   "An April Day" [19]
           "Supplication" [20]
p. 3   "Ego" [6]
p. 4   "Is This the Price of Love?" [5]
p. 5   "Dreams" [7]
p. 6   "And What Shall You Say?" [10]
p. 7   "The Band of Gideon" [1]
p. 8   "O, Little David, Play on Your Harp" [12]
p. 9   "Sonnet" [14]
p. 10   "Sonnet to Negro Soldiers" [13]
p. 11   "Sonnet" [15]
p. 12   "November" [23]
[p. 13 (?) "Ode to Democracy" [59] (Original ribbon copy lost; top of surviving carbon where page number would appear is cut away.)]
p. 14   "Then I Would Love You" [8]
p. 15   "Remembrance" [22]
p. 16   "Memories" [16]
           "Love" [17]
           "Inconstancy" [18]
p. 17   "The Goal" [21]
p. 18   "To Florence" [24]
p. 19   "I'm A-waiting and A-watching" [9]
p. 20   "Compensation" [25]

Note that "The Deserter" [4] is absent from early "Gideon" and that the title poem [1] appears toward the middle of the collection among poems of black consciousness. It was later moved to first position, displacing "A Prayer" [3] as the opening poem in the published *Gideon*. Also noteworthy is the probable deletion of "Ode to Democracy" [59] from the collection, as discussed above.

Cotter provided a separate title page for the early compilation of his book which reads

THE BAND OF GIDEON
and
OTHER LYRICS
By Joseph S. Cotter, Jr.
oOo-oOo

The early "Gideon" collection was typed on a wine-colored ribbon on the typewriter, probably the family typewriter, that was evidently used for many of Cotter Jr.'s subsequent typescripts and for many of his father's typescripts. Titles of poems on the early "Gideon" typescripts are characteristically typed in all capital letters, underlined, and followed by a period or question mark.[2] Paper of originals and of carbons is typically white wove of a standard size (281 × 219.5 mm) watermarked PRE-EMINENT. Most of the carbons are black. Exceptions as to type of paper or color of carbon are noted in the Apparatus. Two holes are punched about 3 mm from the top and about 42 mm from the left and right edges of the early "Gideon" ribbon and carbon copies. These holes would allow the typescripts to be fastened together with now absent brads or other devices. Another set of two holes, very small and evidently made by a straight pin, occur on the ribbon copies, suggesting that these early "Gideon" typescripts were at one time pinned together. These small holes typically appear at the head of the typescript, just above the title.

Early "Gideon" carbons often reveal corrections typed on the wine-colored ribbon used to produce the original copy. Handwritten corrections and revisions in black ink occur on a number of the ribbon copies as well as carbons of early "Gideon." Revisions of substantives generally appear to be in the hand of Cotter Jr. As specified in the individual Apparatus notes, the entire texts of poems on many of the early "Gideon" typescripts, both ribbon and carbon copies, were crossed out with large exes at some time, perhaps during the revision process from early to later "Gideon."[3]

Later "Gideon" may serve to designate a final group of "Gideon" typescripts which may have been produced in the course of preparations for the publication of *The Band of Gideon* as a book in the early summer of 1918. Texts of the following poems are given on later "Gideon" ribbon copies or carbons or both: "The Band of Gideon" [1], "The Mulatto to His Critics" [2], "A Prayer" [3], "The Deserter" [4], "Is This the Price of Love?" [5], "Ego" [6], "Dreams" [7], "Then I Would Love You" [8], "I'm A-waiting and A-watching" [9], "Memories" [16], "Love" [17], "Inconstancy" [18], "An April Day" [19], "Supplication" [20], and "The Goal" [21]. These poems are listed here in the order as published in *The Band of Gideon* and in this edition. The later "Gideon" typescripts were found randomly placed among the Cotter papers, and they bear no page numbers. A listing of specific ribbon copies and carbons of later "Gideon" texts of individual poems is given in the Apparatus. The typescript of the introduction by Cale Young Rice to *The Band of Gideon* is with the later "Gideon" typescripts at the Western Branch Library, tending to confirm the hypothesis that these late typescripts were made in preparation for the 1918 book. It may be noted, too, that when later "Gideon" poems are typed two or three to a page, as with "The Mulatto to His Critics" [2] and "A Prayer" [3] on one page and "Memories" [16], "Love" [17], and "Inconstancy" [18] on another, the sequence of poems is always the same as that in the published *Gideon*.

While readings of poems of the early "Gideon" compilation at times differ markedly from those of *Gideon* as published, later "Gideon" typescript readings are generally close to versions of poems published in *Gideon*. The listing in the Apparatus of variants for the title poem [1] provides an interesting example of differences between an early and later "Gideon" text. As in the case of the early "Gideon" ribbon and carbon typescripts, revisions of substantives on some of the later "Gideon" typescripts in what appears to be Cotter Jr.'s hand attest to the poet's attention to the later "Gideon" materials, though no documents presently available prove the identity of the typist of any of the Cotter Jr. typescripts. Unlike the early

"Gideon" compilation, there is no extant later "Gideon" title page, and there is no consistent pattern of punch or pin holes linking the later "Gideon" typescripts together. Apart from the closeness of readings of the poems of later "Gideon" to published *Gideon*, there are other unifying characteristics of the final group of "Gideon" typescripts that may be mentioned. The appearance of titles of the poems of later "Gideon" is typically like that on the early "Gideon" typescripts; that is, titles are in all capitals, underlined, and followed by a period or question mark.[4] Paper of later "Gideon" typescripts is uniformly white, wove, unwatermarked typing paper, typed on one side of the leaf only.

Three sets of typescripts of poems [26–58] eventually published in the third quarter 1920 and the second quarter 1921 *A.M.E. Zion Quarterly Review* comprise the final substantial body of typed material of Cotter Jr. at the Western Branch Library in Louisville. Each of these typescript sets carries the title "Out of the Shadows" on a separate title page, and for purposes of brief reference I have designated these typescript groups "Shadows"-A, "Shadows"-B, and "Shadows"-C. A separate typed sheet bearing texts of two of the posthumously published poems, "To ———" [50] and "Moloch" [51], is designated "Shadows"-D. The kinship of these final typescript groups is evident in their overall appearance[5] and content; further details are given in the following specific discussion of each group.

The "Shadows"-A group consists of nineteen leaves typed on one side only. The "Out of the Shadows" sonnet sequence [26–44] appears on the first through twelfth pages, typed one or two sonnets to a page. The group of fourteen poems [45–58] published under the rubric "Poems" in the second quarter 1921 *Zion Quarterly* appears on the thirteenth through nineteenth pages, one to four poems to a page. The first through twelfth pages, those carrying the sonnet sequence, bear no page numbers. The thirteenth through eighteenth pages bear page numbers 1–7 penciled in arabic numerals in the upper left corner of pages. The first eighteen typescript pages of "Shadows"-A are wine-colored ribbon copies on unwatermarked, white, wove paper. The final typescript page is a black carbon on unwatermarked onionskin of a lost ribbon copy of the poem "Theodore Roosevelt" [58], the final poem of the two groups posthumously published in the *Zion Quarterly*. The widely varying sizes of the leaves of the "Shadows"-A group of typescripts are given in the Apparatus along with additional descriptive details.

The first through eighteenth leaves of the "Shadows"-A group are punched horizontally at the top with two holes, set in about 3 mm from the top edge, 59 mm from the left edge, and 77 mm from the right edge, to accommodate metal brads or fasteners which originally held the typescripts to a light green construction paper back cover (298 irreg. × 231 mm). When I studied the typescripts in July 1986, the metal fasteners still held the twelfth through seventeenth leaves to the green construction paper back; the first through eleventh leaves, with punched holes mostly torn through, were paper-clipped in place. The last leaf, carrying the carbon copy of "Theodore Roosevelt" [58], appears not to have been punched with holes; it is tipped in at the end of the set of typescripts. If the "Shadows"-A typescripts ever had a front cover, it is now lost.

The separate title page of "Shadows"-A is written entirely in pencil in the hand, apparently, of Cotter Sr. In the center, beneath a horizontal line, "Out of the Shadows" is written; "By Joseph S. Cotter, Jr." follows below the title. "Out of the Shadows- | An Unfinished Sonnet-Sequence." written at the top of the title page refers, of course, to the nineteen-poem sequence [26–44] which makes up the first section of the compilation. The typed sonnets are numbered with penciled arabic numerals, typically written in the left margin of the typescript, which correspond to the numbers of the sonnets as published in the *Zion Quarterly*. The arrangement and numbering of the sonnets in "Shadows"-A is a point of interest in the study of the genesis of this significant modern Afro-American sonnet sequence, and is given in the following table (page numbers are given for descriptive purposes; they do not appear on the sonnet sequence pages of the "Shadows"-A compilation):

Page	Sonnets
1	I [26]
2	II [27], III [28]
3	IV [29], V [30]
4	VI [31]
5	VII [32], VIII [33]

6	IX [34], X [35]
7	XI [36], XII [37]
8	XIII [38], XIV [39]
9	XVI [41]
10	XV [40], XVII [42]
11	XVIII [43]
12	XIX [44]

A penciled "16" in the space between the fifteenth and seventeenth sonnets on the tenth typescript page signals the ultimate position of Sonnet XVI [41] in the sequence, which may well have been inserted later between what then became the eighth and tenth pages. The significance of this late addition of Sonnet XVI to the "Shadows"-A compilation is not completely clear. The sonnet may have been accidentally and temporarily omitted in the typing process and then inserted. Or Cotter may have withheld the ultimate placement of this crucial sonnet while he made his final deliberations on the overall structure of the sequence. The notion that the final placement of Sonnet XVI came late as Cotter deliberated on the overall arrangement and structuring of the sequence may be supported by the fact that Sonnet XVI is one of three sonnets of the sequence absent from the Louisville school-tablet compilation.[6]

It is virtually certain that the poet's father assisted substantially in the compilation of the "Shadows"-A set of typescripts. The title page appears to have been written in the father's hand, and one short, four-line poem of the eclectic group following the sonnet sequence, "I Shall Not Die" [48], was actually copied in pencil in what seems to be Cotter Sr.'s hand at the bottom of the typescript page. In addition to the handwriting of the father, some of the "Shadows"-A typescripts carry substantive penciled revisions which appear to be in the hand of Cotter Jr., indicating his probable attention to the compilation. Noteworthy are revisions in the young poet's hand in the left margin of the "Shadows"-A typescript of Sonnet XVI suggestive of Cotter Jr.'s attention to that text which may have been added later to that first typed version of the sequence, as discussed above.

The "Shadows"-B and -C typescripts are black carbons on white, unwatermarked onionskin (268 × 204 mm) produced simultaneously during the typing of a now lost original. The "Shadows"-B group includes seventeen leaves typed on one side only with one to four poems to a page; these pages carry no page numbers. "Shadows"-B provides copies of the nineteen "Out of the Shadows" sonnets [26–44] and all of the fourteen poems [45–58] eventually published in the second quarter 1921 *Zion Quarterly*. "Shadows"-C, essentially similar to "Shadows"-B in most other important respects, consists of only sixteen leaves: The leaf that would have corresponded to the thirteenth leaf of "Shadows"-B is absent from "Shadows"-C, and thus copies of "Moloch" [51] and "Rain Music" [52], the poems that would have appeared on the missing page, do not appear in "Shadows"-C. Both the "Shadows"-B and -C sets carry a separate title page with the roughly centered title "Out of the Shadows" typed above "By Joseph S. Cotter, Jr." Two holes are punched horizontally near the top of the "Shadows"-B and -C typescript leaves to accommodate metal fasteners or brads which are in place on both sets of typescripts. On "Shadows"-B the holes are set in about 72 mm from the left and right edges and about 9 mm down from the top of the pages. On "Shadows"-C the holes are punched about 57 mm in on the left edge, 68 mm in from the right edge, and about 9 mm down from the top. The metal fasteners attach the "Shadows"-B typescripts to a light green construction paper back cover (281.5 × 230 mm); there is no front cover. "Shadows"-C lacks both front and back covers. "Shadows"-B and -C bear hand-written, black ink corrections of accidentals. The black ink deletions of stanzas of "To ———" [50] and of "Moloch" [51] are described in the Apparatus. Since there are no handwritten words on either "Shadows"-B or -C, it is impossible to determine whose hand went over these typescripts with the fountain pen.

The unified arrangement of poems [26–58] under the single title "Out of the Shadows" that "Shadows"-B and -C present suggests that these typescripts may have been prepared as copy for a second book by Cotter Jr. If so, the book would have included thirty-three poems — the nineteen poems of the sonnet sequence [26–44] plus the eclectic group of fourteen poems [45–58] following. Yet such a book was not to be. It is tempting to surmise that the missing rib-bon copy of which the "Shadows"-B and -C typescripts are carbons, originally intended as copy for the second book, was ultimately sent to the *Zion Quarterly* as copy for the third quarter 1920 and second quarter 1921 poetry sections of that journal. Cotter Sr.'s interest in the posthumous publication of his son's poetry and the probability that it was the elder Cotter who sent Cotter Jr.'s poems to the *Zion Quarterly* for publication are discussed in the introductory essay to this edition.

The "Shadows"-D typescript, a single page carrying texts of "To ———" [50] and "Moloch" [51], is a black carbon of a lost original on white, unwatermarked, wove paper (276 × 216.5 mm). "Shadows"-D resembles the "Shadows"-B and -C typescripts in a general way, but the fact that stanzas of "To ———" and "Moloch" which are hand-deleted on "Shadows"-A, -B, and -C texts of the poems are entirely absent from the "Shadows"-D texts suggests that the "Shadows"-D texts were prepared at a later time (see Apparatus on texts of "To ———" [50] and "Moloch" [51]).

Published Texts

Published texts of Cotter's poems that appeared in his lifetime include *The Band of Gideon and Other Lyrics*, published by the Cornhill Company, Boston, June 26, 1918, and the single poem from *The Band of Gideon*, "Sonnet to Negro Soldiers" [13], published in the *Crisis*, volume 16, June 1918, p. 64. In the year after Cotter's death, his "Out of the Shadows: An Unfinished Sonnet-Sequence" of nineteen sonnets [26–44] was published in the *A.M.E. Zion Quarterly Review*, volume 31,[7] third quarter, 1920, pp. 54–59. The following year fourteen "Poems" [45–58] were published in the *A.M.E. Zion Quarterly Review*, volume 32, second quarter, 1921, pp. 56–57. Cotter Sr., working from the authority of surviving manuscripts and knowledge of his son's intentions, presumably oversaw the publication of his son's poems in the *Zion Quarterly*. These *Band of Gideon*, *Crisis*, and *Zion Quarterly* texts are collated in this edition with text symbols as listed in the key to text symbols preceding the Apparatus. The published texts consulted and collated during the preparation of this edition are deposited at the following libraries: *The Band of Gideon* (Boston: Cornhill, 1918), Western Branch, Louisville Free Public Library, Louisville, Kentucky; "Sonnet to Negro Soldiers," *Crisis* 16 (1918): 64, Perry-Castaneda Library, University of Texas, Austin;

"Out of the Shadows: An Unfinished Sonnet-Sequence," *A.M.E. Zion Quarterly Review* 31 (1920): 54–59, and "Poems," *A.M.E. Zion Quarterly Review* 32 (1921): 56–57, Schomburg Center for Research in Black Culture, New York City.

Later newspaper appearances and reprintings of Cotter's poems in anthologies are not collated.

Copy-texts

Holograph manuscripts serve as copy-texts for forty-six of the sixty-five poems published in this edition. For one poem, "Ego" [6], I have chosen a later "Gideon" typescript as the copy-text because the surviving early-draft manuscript is too distant from the ultimate version of the poem to be practicable. Manuscripts that appear to be in the hand of Joseph Seamon Cotter, Sr., serve as copy-texts for "I Shall Not Die" [48] and "Theodore Roosevelt" [58]. No holograph manuscript sources for these two poems are available, and these manuscripts in the hand of the poet's father are closer to Joseph Seamon Cotter, Jr., than are the poems appearing in the later typescripts and printed versions. I have relied on typescripts for copy-texts of sixteen poems for which there are no extant manuscript sources. One of these typescripts, "To Florence" [24, TS¹], is on one of the signed slips of paper that Cotter may have used to submit his work to journals. None of the other typescripts serving as copy-texts are signed by the poet, and yet they possess authority, in my judgment. Fourteen of the unsigned typescripts are from either the early "Gideon" or later "Gideon" group of typescripts. Within these groups are typescripts which carry substantive revisions and corrections in what appears to be the poet's handwriting. Annotations in the poet's hand do not occur on every typescript of the two groups but do occur on a number of both early and later "Gideon" texts, indicating the poet's attention to these materials. In the case of "Ode to Democracy" [59], the copy-text is a typescript which probably was originally an integral part of the early "Gideon" compilation and was then separated from that group when the poem was deleted from "The Band of Gideon" collection.

The Band of Gideon was published seven months before Cotter's death, and the poet may well have read proof for this carefully produced volume that is generally very close to later "Gideon" type-scripts in its versions of the poetic texts. Yet no documentation of Cotter's actually having read proof is presently available. I have not had to rely on the published *Band of Gideon* nor on the *A.M.E. Zion Quarterly* texts, which appeared after Cotter's death, for copy-texts of any of the poems. It has seemed to me safer to use holograph manuscripts as copy-texts whenever practicable and, when necessary, to rely on typed texts from groups of typescripts that bear evidence of the poet's personal review. When determined to be authoritative revisions by Cotter Jr., readings from post-copy-text manuscripts and typescripts are introduced as emendations to copy-texts. All such emendations of copy-texts and their textual sources, as well as all variant readings of possible authority, are listed in the Apparatus.

Apparatus

Readers will note that I have adapted the plan of the apparatus of the poetry section of Fredson Bowers, ed., *Stephen Crane: Poems and Literary Remains* (Charlottesville: UP of Virginia, 1975) for this Apparatus. The structure allows for the presentation of specific textual notations for each poem together in a unified format.

Following the number assigned to each poem for this edition and the poem's title (or sonnet number), a listing is given of all surviving texts collated for this edition, that is, all texts of possible authority. The texts are listed in what I believe to be chronological order with manuscripts and typescripts for each poem numbered if there are more than one. An asterisk appears before the selected copy-text. For quick reference, texts are very briefly identified or characterized in the initial listing, for example, as a "holograph draft" or of the "early 'Gideon'" compilation.

Following the listing of texts is a record of emendations; any editorial changes from copy-texts, whether of substantives or accidentals, are recorded here. Before the bracket on the emendations list is the line reference and emended reading. Immediately following the bracket is the source of the emendation, and finally, following a semicolon, the actual copy-text reading is given. In the rare instances in which no text symbol immediately follows the bracket, it is to be understood that the emendation is introduced with this edition, that is, with respect to texts collated. The wavy dash symbol "∼" in the emendations list and elsewhere signifies the same word appearing before the bracket and is used in recording differences of punctuation and of other accidentals. The inferior caret "‸" marks the absence of a punctuation mark. The plus sign "+" means that the text cited and all of the following texts as given in the initial listing of texts for a poem provide an identical reading. Thus, the emendation on line 2 of "Is It Because I Am Black?" [11], "2 speech$_\wedge$] TS^1+; ~, MS", could as well have been expressed as "2 speech$_\wedge$] TS$^{1\text{-}3}$, BG; ~, MS".

Following emendations (if any), alterations on manuscripts are recorded. Alterations on typescripts are listed only in instances in which the typescript serves as copy-text. A dagger "†"precedes the line reference number in alterations listings when words or punctuation before the bracket differ from the text of the poem as printed in this edition. Such a difference would be due to the remoteness of an early, pre-copy-text manuscript from the chosen copy-text or to an emendation. The reader should then consult the variants or emendations list on the line in question. Thus, the first alteration listed for the first manuscript of Sonnet VII [32] begins "†4 new-blown]". The dagger indicates that "new-blown" does not occur in the text of the poem as printed in this edition. The reader may then check the variants listings and find the following notation for line 4: "4 crimson . . . grace] new-blown roses, 'mid the comeliness MS^1". We see that "new-blown" occurs as part of a pre-copy-text variant of line 4. The reading before the bracket directs the reader to the location of the passage in question in this edition. In some instances, a difference between an alterations listing and the text of the poem in this edition is due to an emendation, and the reader may check the line in question in the emendations list.

A list of variants which records differences of collated texts from the chosen copy-text appears after the listing of alterations. By consulting the variants list along with the emendations list a reader can reconstruct any of the extant texts of possible authority of any of Cotter's poems. The final item for each poem is a note giving descriptive information and other specific commentary on the manuscripts and typescripts. In the interest of concision, I have endeavored not to repeat general information about manuscripts and typescripts already given in the Textual Commentary. For example, details of sizes and types of paper of relatively uniform typescript sets, such as "Shadows"-B and -C, already given in the Textual Commentary descriptions are not repeated in the Apparatus.

Titles of poems in this edition are set in a uniform fashion. When the wording, capitalization, or punctuation of titles in this edition differs from that of the original manuscripts, the original version of the title is given in the Apparatus notes. The style of titles on typescripts is described in the Typescripts section of the Textual Commentary. All of the titles of poems in published texts collated for this edition are in all capital letters.

Pre-copy-text variations in indentations of lines of poems are not recorded, nor are pre-copy-text variations in stanzaic divisions. Rarely do we see long lines of poems divided for strictly spatial requirements in manuscripts, typescripts, and published texts of Cotter's poems. Such instances of division of lines are not recorded. Throughout the Cotter typescripts both the dash and the hyphen are usually typed "-". The conventional dash " — " and hyphen "-" forms are used in this edition.

In the interest of concision, other practices and conventions have been observed in the Apparatus. Single or double spacing of lines on typescripts is noted only when necessary to distinguish between two otherwise similar typescripts. When the color of typewriter ribbon is unspecified in Apparatus references to original typescripts, the typewriter ribbon is wine-colored. All carbons are black, and all notations on manuscripts are in gray pencil unless otherwise noted. If an Apparatus note on a manuscript or typescript makes no reference to a signature, a date, or a similar inscription, the reader should assume that the document is unsigned, undated, or otherwise unmarked. Indentations of lines of poems edited from manuscripts are set according to the prevailing pattern of the manuscript, and very slight variations within a prevailing manuscript indentation pattern are not recorded. Indentations and spacing of lines on the "Shadows"-A set of typescripts are generally, though not always, indicated by handwritten exes, and occasionally by other marks, rather than by actual spacing. In the Apparatus I have treated these lines marked for indentation as if they were actually indented and spaced as called for by the "x" marks on the "Shadows"-A typescripts unless there is a specific reason to refer to the indentation markings.

Cotter sometimes wrote more than one poem on a manuscript page, he often wrote poems on both sides of leaves, and his typescripts may present as many as four short poems to a page. So that the reader may reconstruct in its entirety any of Cotter's manuscript or typescript leaves, Apparatus notes to texts of poems consistently refer to and cross-reference texts of any other poems above or below on the page or on the reverse side of the manuscript leaf. If no reference is made to the verso of a leaf, it is to be assumed that the verso is blank.

Apparatus notations of manuscript alterations and other descriptive notes on manuscripts sometimes refer to inscriptions in a "heavier hand" or to words "traced over" or "reinforced." Such information is never meant to imply a hand other than that of Joseph Seamon Cotter, Jr. Evidently Cotter often carefully traced over letters on his manuscripts, occasionally in purple ink, presumably to guarantee his intended readings of the words of his poems. Whenever the editor deems an inscription to be in a hand other than that of Cotter Jr., explicit mention is made and identification of the "other hand" is attempted, insofar as possible. In most cases, the "other hand" will be that of the poet's father, Joseph Seamon Cotter, Sr.

Key to Text Symbols of Collated Published Work of Joseph Seamon Cotter, Jr.

AME 1920   "Out of the Shadows: An Unfinished Sonnet-Sequence," *A.M.E. Zion Quarterly Review* 31 (third quarter 1920): 54–59.

AME 1921   "Poems," *A.M.E. Zion Quarterly Review* 32 (second quarter 1921): 56–57.

BG   *The Band of Gideon and Other Lyrics* (Boston: Cornhill, 1918).

Cr   "Sonnet to Negro Soldiers," *Crisis* 16 (June 1918): 64.

Abbreviations Used in Apparatus

h. sp.	head space
illeg.	illegible
irreg.	irregular
MS	manuscript
mm	millimeters
t. sp.	tail space

t.o.	typed over
TS	typescript
w.o.	handwritten over

Some Symbols Used in Apparatus

⟨ ⟩   Angle brackets mark sections of transcribed manuscript material removed by a tear in the manuscript.

| One vertical line indicates single line division.

‖   Two vertical lines indicate double line division.

Other symbols are explained in the introduction to the Apparatus.

The Band of Gideon and Other Lyrics

1. THE BAND OF GIDEON

TS¹, early "Gideon," ribbon; TS², carbon of TS¹; *TS³, later "Gideon," blue carbon; BG

Emendations: 6 steed.] TS¹⁻², BG; ~, TS³
29 soul,"] BG; ~ ∧ " TS¹; ~", TS²⁻³ (*comma added by hand in black ink* TS²)

TS³ Alterations: †6 steed,] *comma may be t.o. erasure*
21 the] "t" *t.o. erasure*
†29 soul",] *comma added by hand, black ink*

Variants: 1, 19, 39 band] Band TS¹⁻²
1 sky,] ~∧ TS² (*comma handwritten on* TS¹)
2 war-cry] shrill war-cry TS¹⁻²
3 trump's] trumpet TS¹⁻²
4 vengeful] vengeant TS¹⁻²
5, 14, 23, 32, 41 black] jet-black TS¹⁻²
8, 17, 26, 35, 44 With each strong] When done each TS¹⁻²
9, 18, 27, 36, 45 the Lord and Gideon."] Gideon and the Lord." TS¹⁻²
10 temples] their temples TS¹⁻²
11 reasons] their reasons TS¹⁻²
12 And] Then TS¹⁻²
12 shame,] ~∧ TS¹ (*comma added by hand, black ink* TS²)
20 baleful] a baleful TS¹⁻²
20 eye,] ~. TS¹⁻²; ~; BG
21 In] Then in TS¹⁻²

22 burning] the burning TS$^{1-2}$
29 mercy] mercey TS^1 (TS^2 *is hand corrected in black ink*)
31 God.] ∼, TS$^{1-2}$
38 met,] ∼. TS$^{1-2}$
40 strike] strick TS$^{1-2}$

Note: TS$^{1-2}$ are on paper watermarked PRE-EMINENT. On both, the whole text of the poem is crossed out in pencil, and both bear the typed page number "7" in the upper right corner. TS^3 is on unwatermarked paper (279 × 215 mm).

2. THE MULATTO TO HIS CRITICS

*MS, holograph; TS^1, ribbon on slip, signed in black ink; TS^2, early "Gideon," ribbon; TS^3, carbon of TS^2; TS^4, second carbon of TS^2; TS^5, later "Gideon," carbon of lost original; TS^6, blue carbon of same lost original as TS^5; BG

Emendation: 3 I (*no indentation*)] TS^1+; *appears to be indented one space* MS

MS Alterations: 2 what] "t" *w.o. illeg.*
5 Red Man] *first stroke of* "M" *w.o. to change* "m" *to* "M"
8 the kindly] "e" *w.o.* "e"?
9 skin] "s" *w.o. illeg.*

Variant: 5 Celt$_\wedge$] ∼, TS$^{5-6}$

Note: The MS, on the front of the third ring-binder leaf, bears a penciled "5." in the upper left margin, the abbreviation "Pub." in the upper right margin, and a check mark to the right below the poem. MS title is written "The Mulatto To His Critics", with "to" altered to "To" and "r" written over an illegible letter. On the back of the manuscript leaf are holograph copies of "Immortality" [45, MS^2] and "A Woman at Her Husband's Grave" [46, MS^3].

TS^1 is on wove paper (109–113 irreg. × 140 mm) with a partial watermark BERKSHIRE ‖ SOUVENIR BOND ‖ U.S.A. TS$^{2-4}$, on PRE-EMINENT watermarked paper, bear page number "1" in the upper right corner, and are typed on the lower half of the page following typescript of "A Prayer" [3, TS$^{2-4}$]. In the space between poems is a row of three typed asterisks. The entire text of the poem on TS$^{2-3}$ is canceled in pencil with a large ex that also crosses out text of "A Prayer" at top of page. To the left of the first line of "The Mulatto" on TS[4] is a penciled "1" which corresponds to a penciled "2" to the left of the first line of "A Prayer." These numbers suggest an intention to reverse the order of the two poems in the compilation. The reversed order does indeed occur on later typescripts TS[5-6], on which "The Mulatto" is typed above "A Prayer." The new sequence is seen in the published *Band of Gideon*, with "The Mulatto" appearing on the page preceding "A Prayer." TS[5-6] are on unwatermarked paper (280 × 215 mm) with a row of four asterisks typed between the two poems.

3. A PRAYER

*MS, holograph; TS[1], ribbon on slip, signed in black ink; TS[2], early "Gideon," ribbon; TS[3], carbon of TS[2]; TS[4], second carbon of TS[2]; TS[5], later "Gideon," carbon of lost original; TS[6], blue carbon of same lost original as TS[5]; BG

Emendation: 3 ceiling$_\wedge$] TS[1]+; ~, MS

MS Alterations: 1 bed] *preceded by canceled* "my"
3 ceiling] "ei" *w.o. illeg.*

Variants: 1 bed,] my bed$_\wedge$ TS[1]; my bed, TS[2-4]
2 back;] ~, TS[1]
4 things—] ~. TS[1-6]
5 gay-voiced] ~$_\wedge$~ TS[2-3] (*hyphen added by hand* TS[4])
7 moonlit] moon-lit TS[1-6]
8 motherhood] mother-hood TS[1] (*hyphen squeezed in by hand*); Motherhood TS[2]+

Note: "Pub." is written above the title, and there are two check marks at the foot of MS, which is on the front of the tenth ring-binder leaf. The title "A Prayer" is written over the erased title "Dream Children". On the back of the manuscript leaf is a holograph copy of "Africa" [57, MS].

TS[1] is on a small piece of paper (105–102 irreg. × 142–140 irreg. mm) bearing no watermark. On TS[2-4], "A Prayer" occupies the upper half of the page, above typescript of "The Mulatto to His Critics" [2, TS[2-4]]. These early "Gideon" typescripts carry page number "1" typed in the upper right corner and a row of three asterisks mid-page between the poems. They are on PRE-EMINENT watermarked paper. On both TS[2-3], "A Prayer" is canceled in pencil with large exes which also cross out "The Mulatto" below. On TS⁴, a penciled "2" to the left of "A Prayer" corresponding to a penciled "1" to the left of "The Mulatto," which appears below "A Prayer" on the typescript, suggests Cotter's intention to reverse the order of appearance of the two poems in *Gideon*. On the later typescripts, TS⁵⁻⁶, "The Mulatto" does appear above "A Prayer" on the page, presaging the sequence in the published *Band of Gideon*. A row of four asterisks separates the two poems on the two late typescripts, which are on unwatermarked paper (280 × 215 mm).

4. THE DESERTER

*MS, holograph, signed; TS¹, later "Gideon," black ribbon; TS², later "Gideon," blue carbon of lost original; BG

Emendation: 3 brought] TS¹+; brot MS

MS Alterations: 1 or whence] *added above line with caret*
6 Nor . . . may] *interlined above deleted* "The path o'er which he"
9 For . . . hope] *follows canceled line* "For love is life and love is light"

Variants: 2, 4, 6, 8, 10, 12 [*indented two spaces*]] *indented four spaces* TS¹⁻²
3 love,] ∼ₐ TS¹+
4 going—]∼, TS¹+
5 backₐ] ∼, TS¹+
6 rove,] ∼; TS¹+
9 hopeₐ] ∼, TS¹+
10 fled,] ∼; TS¹+

Note: The MS, on torn, blue-ruled, yellowish-brown pad paper (272 × 202 mm, 52 mm h. sp.), carries no title. (See illustration.) Title supplied from TS¹+. TS¹⁻² are on unwatermarked typing paper (279.5 × 215 mm).

5. IS THIS THE PRICE OF LOVE?

*MS, holograph; TS¹, early "Gideon," ribbon; TS², carbon of TS¹; TS³, later "Gideon," carbon of lost original; TS⁴, second carbon of same lost original as TS³; BG

Emendations: 6 cheer] TS¹+; cherr MS
7, 15 Thou] TS³+; God MS, TS¹⁻²

7, 15 hearest] TS³+; hears me MS, TS¹⁻²

MS Alterations: 5 Never] "r" *w.o. illeg.*
†6 cherr] "rr" *w.o. illeg.*
13 song] "s" *w.o. illeg.*

Variants: 2, 4, 6, 10, 12, 14 [*indented two spaces*]] *indented three spaces* TS¹⁻²;
   indented four spaces TS³⁻⁴
7, 15 above,] ~ₐ TS¹⁻²
13 Never (*no indentation*)] *indented one space* BG

Note: "Pub." is written in the upper left corner, and there appear to be two check marks to the right below the poem on MS, which is on the front of the eighth ring-binder leaf. MS title is written "Is This The Price Of Love?" On the back of the manuscript leaf is a holograph copy of "Love's Demesne" [56, MS²].

TS¹⁻², on PRE-EMINENT watermarked paper, bear a typed page number "4" in the upper right corner. The whole text of the poem is exed out on TS¹⁻². A row of five asterisks typed between stanzas is deleted in pencil on TS¹ and erased on TS². TS³⁻⁴ are on unwatermarked typing paper (279 × 215 mm).

6. EGO

MS, holograph draft; TS¹, early "Gideon," ribbon; TS², carbon of TS¹;
   *TS³, later "Gideon," carbon of lost original; TS⁴, second carbon of
   same lost original as TS³; BG

Emendation: 19 above heaven,] MS, TS² (*comma added by hand, black ink*),
   BG; ~ ~ₐ TS¹, TS³⁻⁴

MS Alterations: 3 whirling] *follows deleted word,* "their"?
†10 decline] *interlined above canceled* "fall"
15 Dream] *last stroke of* "m" *appears to be w.o.* "s"; *reading might be* "Dreams"
17 eternity's] "y's" *in darker pencil over* "ies"

TS³ Alterations: 2 night] *t.o. erasure*
3 glamour,] *black ink comma hand-formed from prior illeg. punctuation mark*
9 Stars] "a" *added by hand, black ink*
13 from aeon] "a" *t.o. possible* "x"
15 that,] *comma added by hand, black ink*

15 starward,] *comma added by hand, black ink*
20 death] "d" *t.o. illeg. letter*

Variants: 2, 4, 6, 8, 10, 12, 14, 16, 18, 20 [*lines indented four spaces*]] *indented two spaces* BG
3 glamour,] glamour ⟨ ⟩ MS (*end of line punctuation indeterminable because of tear on MS*); ~_∧ TS[1-2]
4 All unto all] Each after each MS, TS[1-2]
7 grievings_∧] ~, MS
8 a passionless] abysmil MS
10 Rising or falling or pausing a span,] Rise and decline but to rise again, MS
11 replying_∧] ~, BG
13 aeon to aeon,] aeon to aeon_∧ MS; æon to æon, BG
14 dust,] ~_∧ MS
15 that,] ~_∧ MS, TS[1-2]
15 starward,] starward ⟨ ⟩ MS (*end of line punctuation indeterminable because of tear*); ~_∧ TS[1-2]
16 must."] ~". MS

Note: The MS, on blue-ruled, yellowish-brown pad paper (272 × 200 mm, 53 mm h. sp.), is severely torn, especially along the right side. On the MS, the title, "Ego", is underlined.

TS[1-2], both on paper watermarked PRE-EMINENT, bear the typed page number "3" in the upper right corner. The entire text of the poem is crossed out in pencil on these early "Gideon" typescripts. On the verso of TS[2] there is a typing exercise which fills the whole page. TS[3-4] are on unwatermarked typing paper (279 × 214.5 mm).

7. DREAMS

TS[1], early "Gideon," ribbon; TS[2], carbon of TS[1]; *TS[3], later "Gideon," carbon of lost original; TS[4], second carbon of same lost original as TS[3]; BG

TS³ Alteration: 9 night] "n" *t.o. erasure*

Variants: 2, 4, 8, 10 [*lines indented five spaces*]] *indented two spaces* BG
6 earth or fancy's] realness or fanciful TS[1-2]
7 There is naught,] Oft I sit_∧ TS[1-2]

9 lands] the lands TS$^{1-2}$
9 night,] $\sim_\wedge$ TS$^{1-2}$
10 Or] And the TS$^{1-2}$
10 the sunswept sky,] a sun-swept sky. TS$^{1-2}$
11 For countless spirits within me] And spirits of yore in my soul do TS$^{1-2}$
12 With] In TS$^{1-2}$
12 dark hell] darkness of hell TS$^{1-2}$

Note: TS$^{1-2}$ are on paper watermarked PRE-EMINENT; on each, the entire text of the poem is crossed out in pencil. A typed page number "5" appears in the upper right corner of TS$^{1-2}$. TS$^{3-4}$ are both on unwatermarked typing paper (279 × 214.5 mm).

8. THEN I WOULD LOVE YOU

*MS, holograph; TS^1, ribbon on slip, signed in black ink; TS^2, early "Gideon," ribbon; TS^3, carbon of TS^2; TS^4, later "Gideon," black ribbon, single-spaced; TS^5, later "Gideon," black ribbon, double-spaced; BG

Emendations: [*stanzas not numbered*]] TS^1+; *numbered* "I" *and* "II" MS
20 full,] TS^1+ ("full" *written above deleted* "red" *in black ink in what appears to be Cotter's hand; comma inserted in same black ink* TS^1); red, MS

MS Alterations: 10 sips;] *upper part of semicolon reinforced or w.o. prior mark*
13 come] "m" *w.o. illeg.*
20 lips] "s" *appears to be added*
23 would] "u" *w.o. illeg.*

Variants: 2 clear,] $\sim_\wedge$ TS^4+
4 noontide] noon-tide TS^1+
5 dark,] $\sim_\wedge$ TS^4+
7 stirs] sturs TS^3 (*error hand corrected in black ink on ribbon copy* TS^2)
8 And$_\wedge$] $\sim$, TS^4+
9 bud,] $\sim_\wedge$ TS^1+
10 sips;] $\sim$. TS$^{1-3}$; $\sim$, TS^4+
11 you.] $\sim$, TS^1+
13 But$_\wedge$] $\sim$, TS^5+
16 Western] western TS^1+
17 hair,] $\sim_\wedge$ TS^4+

17 wind-caught‸] ∼ - ∼, TS³ (*comma added by hand, probably in pencil*)

18–19 And . . . wrought;] *lines omitted* TS³ (*restored by hand in black ink on ribbon copy* TS²)

21 slender] slendor TS³ (*error hand corrected in black ink on* TS²)

21 midst an] mid a TS⁵+

22 me,] ∼. TS¹⁻³; ∼! TS⁴⁻⁵

23 Then] When TS³ (*error hand corrected in black ink on* TS²)

Note: Written on the front of the fifth ring-binder leaf, the MS carries the notation "Pub." written in the upper right corner and a check mark in the lower right margin. MS title is written "Then I Would Love You.", with "w" altered to "W" and "ve" written over illegible letters. On the back of the manuscript leaf is a holograph copy of "Night Winds" [47, MS²].

On wove paper (238–232 irreg. × 138–140 irreg. mm), TS¹ bears a partial watermark of BERKSHIRE ‖ SOUVENIR BOND ‖ U.S.A. At the top of TS¹ Cotter signed his name and wrote his address by hand in black ink: "2306 Magazine St., | Louisville, Ky." TS² is on typing paper (280 × 216 mm) with no discernible watermark; its carbon, TS³, is on OLD MILL watermarked typing paper (280 × 216 mm). Both TS²⁻³ carry the typed page number "14", and on both the poem is canceled with large, penciled exes. TS⁴⁻⁵ are on unwatermarked white paper (275 × 215.5 mm and 267 irreg. × 215 mm, respectively). Two small holes above the title suggest that TS⁵ was once pinned with a straight pin.

9. I'M A-WAITING AND A-WATCHING

TS¹, early "Gideon," ribbon; TS², carbon of TS¹; *TS³, later "Gideon," blue carbon of lost original; BG

Emendation: 11 heavens'] BG; heaven's TS¹⁻³

TS³ Alterations: 1 I'm] *apostrophe and first part of* "m" *added in pencil*
2 sun] "u" *t.o.* "i"
3 fair] "a" *t.o.* "i"
7 of] "o" *t.o. illeg.*
7 a] *w.o. illeg., black ink*
11 breath,] *comma added by hand, black ink*

Variants: 3 casts] cast TS¹⁻²
6 light,] *on* TS¹ *line ends so close to edge of paper that comma does not appear* (*comma added by hand, black ink* TS²)

8 carol] chanson TS[1-2]
10 shore,] ~,, TS[1]

Note: TS[1-2], typed on paper watermarked PRE-EMINENT, bear page number "19" in the upper right corner. The entire text of the poem is crossed out in pencil on TS[1-2]. TS[3] is on unwatermarked typing paper (279 × 214.5 mm).

10. AND WHAT SHALL YOU SAY?

*MS, holograph; TS[1], ribbon on slip, signed in black ink; TS[2], early "Gideon," ribbon; TS[3], carbon of TS[2]; BG

Emendations: 2 God.] TS[1]+; ~. *or* ~, *could be reading on* MS
5–12 "Lord . . . mocked." (*lines not indented*)] TS[1]+; *indented two spaces* MS

MS Alteration: 13 And] *followed by possible erasure that seems to extend below the line*

Note: The MS, on the front of the seventh ring-binder leaf, bears a check mark below the poem and the abbreviation "Pub." written in the upper right margin. On the back of the leaf is a holograph copy of "Sonnet" [55, MS].

TS[1] is on wove paper (87–93 irreg. × 140–141 irreg. mm) with partial watermark BERKSHIRE ‖ SOUVENIR BOND ‖ U.S.A. TS[2-3], on paper watermarked PRE-EMINENT, occupy the top half of the page, over typescript of "Is It Because I Am Black?" [11, TS[2-3]]. The typed page number "_6" that appears in the upper right corner of TS[2] is erased but visible on TS[3]. A centered row of four asterisks is typed between "And What Shall You Say?" and "Is It Because I Am Black?" on TS[2-3].

11. IS IT BECAUSE I AM BLACK?

*MS, holograph; TS[1], ribbon on slip; TS[2], early "Gideon," ribbon; TS[3], carbon of TS[2]; BG

Emendations: 2 speech‸] TS[1]+; ~, MS
4 cries] TS[1]+; crys MS
8 them‸] TS[1]+; ~, MS
10 black?] TS[1]+; ~. MS

Note: On the front of the sixth ring-binder leaf, the MS has the abbreviation "Pub" written in the upper right margin and a check mark below the poem. On the back of the manuscript leaf is a holograph copy of "To ———" [50, MS].

TS¹, on a small piece of wove paper (216.5 × 139–137 irreg. mm), bears the following penciled notations indicative of editorial review: to the left above the title, "Return | J.F." In the lower left corner, "not enough | point — write some | more stanzas offering | contrast to first | two — in spite of | being black — | Ed." Below the poem is typed, "Joseph Seamon Cotter,Jr., | 2306 Magazine St., | Louisville,Ky." TS²⁻³ are on paper watermarked PRE-EMINENT and occupy the lower half of the page below typescript of "And What Shall You Say?" [10, TS²⁻³]. A typed page number "_6" appears on TS²; "_6" is partly erased but still visible on TS³. A comma typed in error appears between lines 7 and 8, TS²⁻³. A row of four asterisks is typed between "And What Shall You Say?" and "Is It Because I Am Black?" on TS²⁻³.

12. O, LITTLE DAVID, PLAY ON YOUR HARP

*TS¹, early "Gideon," ribbon; TS², carbon of TS¹; BG

Emendation: 32 "Kultur's"] BG; "Kultur's‸ TS¹⁻²

TS¹ Alterations: 1 O *(designated "Italics")] probably t.o. erasure*

1–6, 37–42 *two parallel lines drawn vertically by hand in black ink just to left of opening and closing stanzas and hand printed "Italics" centered in margin to left of each set of lines give direction to italicize*

2 harp *(designated "Italics")]* "h" *t.o. erasure*

2 golden *(designated "Italics")]* "o" *t.o. illeg.*

3 Jewry *(designated "Italics")]* "J" *t.o. illeg.;* "ry" *t.o. erasure*

6 play *(designated "Italics")]* "p" *probably t.o. erasure*

12 over all] "a" *may be t.o. illeg.; erased word* "all" *visible following*

18 World-creature . . . no] "d-creature . . . no" *t.o. erasure*

29 Flanders'] "s" *underlined in pencil and apostrophe added*

42 David *(designated "Italics")]* "i" *t.o. illeg.*

Variants: 1–6, 37–42 [*lines designated "Italics"*]] *lines not italicized* TS²+

1, 6, 37, 42 O,] ∼‸ BG

2 strings‸ *(designated "Italics")]* ∼, TS² *(comma handwritten in black ink; word not italicized)*

17 Nurtured] Nutured BG

29 Flanders'] $\sim_{\wedge}$ TS² +

Note: TS¹⁻² are on paper watermarked PRE-EMINENT. Page number " '8" appears in upper right corner of TS¹; " '8" mostly erased on TS². The first word of the title is not set off with a comma in the published *Band of Gideon* (BG) text.

13. SONNET TO NEGRO SOLDIERS

*TS¹, early "Gideon," ribbon; TS², carbon of TS¹; Cr; BG

Emendation: 2 unafraid] Cr+; unfraid TS¹⁻²

TS¹ Alterations: 1 unto] "u" *handwritten over illeg., black ink;* "un" *pencil underlined*
4 hand] *small hole in paper following, probably from erasure*
5 arméd] *accent mark added by hand, black ink*

Variants: 4 hand$_{\wedge}$] $\sim$, TS² (*comma added by hand, black ink*), BG
5 arméd] armed TS² +
8+ [*no space*]] *octave and sestet spaced as separate stanzas* Cr
10 resurrection morn] Resurrection Morn Cr
11 Faith$_{\wedge}$] $\sim$, TS² (*comma added by hand, black ink*), Cr+
11 benign$_{\wedge}$] $\sim$, TS² (*comma added by hand, black ink*), Cr+
12 brows] blows Cr
13 prejudice] Prejudice Cr

Note: TS¹⁻², on paper watermarked PRE-EMINENT, carry page number "10" typed in the upper right corner. The *Crisis* text (Cr) is titled "A SONNET TO NEGRO SOLDIERS" and carries the dedication "*Dedicated to the Ninety-Second Division, U. S. National Army*" just above the poem.

14. SONNET

*TS¹, early "Gideon," ribbon; TS², carbon of TS¹; BG

TS¹ Alterations: 6 wind's] *apostrophe t.o. erased* "s"
7 One] "O" *w.o. typed* "o", *black ink*
8 Thee] "T" *t.o. illeg.*
12 prayers] "p" *t.o. illeg.*

13 of] "f" *t.o. illeg.*
13 him] *followed by erased punctuation mark*
13 cry,] *comma added by hand, black ink*

Variant: 13 him$_\wedge$] ~, BG

Note: TS$^{1-2}$ are on paper watermarked PRE-EMINENT. TS^1 has page number "9" typed in the upper right corner; "9" on TS^2 is faint, evidently erased. A row of seven asterisks above a row of two asterisks is centered below the poem on TS$^{1-2}$.

15. SONNET

*TS^1, early "Gideon," ribbon; TS^2, carbon of TS^1; BG

Emendation: 3 That (*indented two spaces*)] BG; *indented one space* TS$^{1-2}$

TS^1 Alterations: 3 fate] "f" *added by hand in black ink over erasure, probably erased* "F"
3 bind] *t.o. erased word*
13 Man] "M" *t.o.* "m"

Variants: 7 Valley] valley BG
7 Moaning Wind] moaning wind BG
13 Man] man BG

Note: TS$^{1-2}$ are on paper watermarked PRE-EMINENT. TS^1 carries page number "11" typed in the upper right corner. On the carbon, TS^2, "11" is erased but visible. An erased row of four asterisks is centered in the space between the octave and sestet on typescripts.

16. MEMORIES

TS^1, early "Gideon," ribbon; TS^2, carbon of TS^1; *TS^3, later "Gideon," black ribbon; TS^4, blue carbon of TS^3; BG

TS^3 Alterations: 4 sea,] *comma added by hand in black ink*
6 Bedecked] "B" *t.o. illeg.*

Variants: 2, 4, 6, 8 [*indented four spaces*]] *indented two spaces* BG
8 brought] brot TS$^{1-2}$

Note: TS[1-2], on paper watermarked PRE-EMINENT, carry page number "16" in the upper right corner and a row of seven typed asterisks centered at the foot. "Memories" appears at the top of the page on TS[1-4], above "Love" [17, TS[1-4]] mid-page, and "Inconstancy" [18, TS[1-4]] below "Memories" and "Love." The three poems are crossed out in pencil on both TS[1-2]. TS[3-4] are both on unwatermarked typing paper; TS[3], 279 × 214.5 mm, TS[4], 280 × 215 mm.

17. LOVE

TS[1], early "Gideon," ribbon; TS[2], carbon of TS[1]; *TS[3], later "Gideon," black ribbon; TS[4], blue carbon of TS[3]; BG

Variants: 2, 4 [*lines indented four spaces*]] *indented two spaces* BG

Note: On paper watermarked PRE-EMINENT, TS[1-2] bear page number "16" in the upper right corner and a row of seven typed asterisks centered at foot. A typescript of "Memories" [16, TS[1-4]] appears above "Love," and a typescript of "Inconstancy" [18, TS[1-4]] is below "Love" on TS[1-4]. On both TS[1-2] the three poems are crossed out in pencil. TS[3-4], both on unwatermarked typing paper, are 279 × 214.5 mm and 280 × 215 mm respectively.

18. INCONSTANCY

TS[1], early "Gideon," ribbon; TS[2], carbon of TS[1]; *TS[3], later "Gideon," black ribbon; TS[4], blue carbon of TS[3]; BG

Variants: 2, 4, 6, 8 [*lines indented five spaces*]] *indented two spaces* BG
8 ∧Love∧∧] "∼", TS[1-2]

Note: On PRE-EMINENT watermarked paper, TS[1-2] carry page number "16" in the upper right corner and a row of seven typed asterisks centered at foot. "Inconstancy" appears below typescript of "Memories" [16, TS[1-4]] in first position, and "Love" [17, TS[1-4]] mid-page, on TS[1-4]. The three poems are crossed out in pencil on TS[1-2]. Both on unwatermarked typing paper, TS[3-4] are 279 × 214.5 mm and 280 × 215 mm respectively.

19. AN APRIL DAY

TS¹, early "Gideon," ribbon; TS², greenish-blue carbon of TS¹; TS³, later "Gideon," black ribbon; *TS⁴, later "Gideon," black ribbon; TS⁵, later "Gideon," carbon of lost original; BG

TS⁴ Alteration: 6 Upon] "n" *may be t.o. illeg.*

Variants: 1 this₍₎] ~, TS³
1 think] trow TS¹⁻²
2, 4, 6, 8 [*indented four spaces*]] *indented two spaces* BG

Note: TS¹⁻², both on typing paper watermarked OLD MILL (280 × 216 mm), carry typed page number "2" in the upper right corner. On TS¹⁻⁵ "An April Day" appears above "Supplication" [20, TS¹⁻⁵]. On both TS¹⁻² the texts of the two poems are exed out in pencil. The later "Gideon" typescripts TS³⁻⁵ are all on unwatermarked typing paper, 279.5 × 215 mm.

20. SUPPLICATION

TS¹, early "Gideon," ribbon; TS², greenish-blue carbon of TS¹; TS³, later "Gideon," black ribbon; *TS⁴, later "Gideon," black ribbon; TS⁵, later "Gideon," carbon of lost original; BG

TS⁴ Alterations: 2 the endless fight,] "the" *t.o. illeg.*; "endless fight," *appears to be t.o. erasure*
4 night] "nigh" *appears to be t.o. erasure*
6 days] "a" *may be t.o. illeg.*

Variants: 1 weary,] ~ — TS¹⁻²
2, 4, 6, 8 [*indented three spaces*]] *indented four spaces* TS⁵; *indented two spaces* BG
2 the endless] this unending TS¹⁻²
3 of waiting] waiting for TS¹⁻²
4 endless] darkest TS¹⁻²
5 That I ask but] But give me TS¹⁻²
6 days that are] the days soon to be TS¹⁻²
8 That I must] Before I TS¹⁻²

Note: TS¹⁻², on OLD MILL watermarked paper (280 × 216 mm), carry typed page number "2" in the upper right corner. "Supplication" appears below "An April Day" [19, TS¹⁻⁵] on TS¹⁻⁵. On both TS¹⁻² the two poems are crossed out with a large penciled ex. TS³⁻⁵ are on unwatermarked typing paper (279.5 × 215 mm).

21. THE GOAL

*MS, holograph; TS¹, ribbon on slip, signed in black ink; TS², early "Gideon," ribbon; TS³, carbon of TS²; TS⁴, later "Gideon," black ribbon; TS⁵, later "Gideon," blue carbon of lost original; BG

Emendations: 2, 4, 6, 8, 10, 14 [*indented two spaces*]] TS¹, TS⁴+; *no indentation* MS, TS²⁻³
9 peace,] TS¹+; ~‿ MS
12, 16 [*indented two spaces*]] TS¹, TS⁵+; *no indentation* MS, TS²⁻⁴
13 Now‿] TS¹+; ~, MS
15 travail,] TS⁴⁻⁵ (*on both, comma handwritten in black ink*), BG; ~‿ MS, TS¹⁻³

MS Alterations: 6 pain] "p" *w.o. erasure in darker pencil or with heavier pressure*
9 found] "f" *w.o. erasure in darker pencil or with heavier pressure*
13 may] "a" *w.o.* "y"?
15 Lord,] *w.o. erasure*

Variants: 2 Surcease‿] ~, TS² (*comma added in pencil*)
3 today] to-day TS¹; to day TS²⁻³, TS⁵
4 tomorrow] to-morrow TS¹

Note: The MS, on the front of the fourth ring-binder leaf, bears these penciled notations: "23" (written over erasure) upper left corner; "Pub.", upper right corner; and check mark following poem. A period follows the title. On the back of the manuscript leaf is a copy of "Looking at a Portrait" [49, MS³].

TS¹ is on wove paper (214–212 irreg. × 134–138 irreg. mm) with a partial watermark BERKSHIRE ‖ SOUVENIR BOND ‖ U.S.A. TS²⁻³, on paper watermarked PRE-EMINENT, carry the typed page number "17". The text of "The Goal" is penciled out with large exes on TS²⁻³. TS⁴ (280 × 216 mm) and TS⁵ (280 × 215.5 mm) are on unwatermarked typing paper.

22. REMEMBRANCE

*MS, holograph; TS^1, ribbon on slip, signed in black ink; TS^2, early "Gideon," ribbon; TS^3, carbon of TS^2; BG

Emendations: 7 loose] TS^2+; lose MS, TS^1
7 their] TS^1+; thier MS
11 too] TS^1+; to MS
16 Heaven] TS^1+; Heav'n MS
18 does] TS^1+; doth MS

MS Alterations: 2 Ah] "A" *w.o. illeg.*
12 The] *canceled* "r"*? extends from* "e"
15 lesion] "e" *appears to be w.o. illeg.*

Variants: 5 all-wise$_\wedge$] ~ - ~, TS^2 (*comma handwritten, black ink*)
9, 18 Fate] fate TS^3+ ("F" *w.o.* "f" *? in each line, black ink* TS^2)

Note: Written on the front of the first ring-binder leaf, the MS carries several penciled notations. Just below a "2." in the upper left corner the word "rewritten" occurs, apparently in Cotter's hand, followed at some distance by a period. "Pub." is written in the upper right head space, and a check mark is in the lower right margin. A copy of "Reward" [53, MS] is on the back of the manuscript leaf.

TS^1 is on a small piece of wove paper (141–136 irreg. × 140 mm) carrying no watermark; TS^2 is on paper (280 × 216 mm) with a possible but indecipherable watermark; and TS^3 is on OLD MILL watermarked paper (280 × 216 mm). A typed page number "15" is in the upper right corner of TS^2; "15" is erased on TS^3.

23. NOVEMBER

*TS, early "Gideon," carbon; BG

TS Alteration: 11 know] "kn" *t.o. illeg.*

Note: TS is on paper partially watermarked PRE-EMINENT; the typed page number "12" is visible, though erased, in the upper right corner.

24. TO FLORENCE

*TS¹, ribbon on slip, signed in black ink; TS², early "Gideon," ribbon; TS³, carbon of TS²; BG

Emendation: 1 Sister *(no indentation)*] TS²+; *indented one space* TS¹

Variants: 7 by] bye TS² ("e" *erased on* TS³)
8 Cloud] cloud BG

Note: Typed on wove paper (98–96 irreg. × 140 mm), TS¹ bears partial watermark BERKSHIRE ‖ SOUVENIR BOND ‖ U.S.A. TS²⁻³ are on PRE-EMINENT watermarked paper. Typed page number "18", in the upper right corner of TS², is erased but visible on TS³ ("L'", typed in error, is discernible above the "18", TS²⁻³). A row of five typed asterisks is centered at foot of early "Gideon" typescripts.

25. COMPENSATION

*TS¹, early "Gideon," ribbon; TS², carbon of TS¹; BG

Emendations: 3 I∧] TS² *(comma erased)*, BG; ∼, TS¹
3 if,] TS² *(comma appears handwritten, black ink)*, BG; ∼∧ TS¹

TS¹ Alteration: 14 But] *w.o. erasure, black ink*

Note: TS¹⁻² are on paper watermarked PRE-EMINENT. The typed page number "20" is in the upper right corner, TS¹; "20" is erased yet visible on TS².

Out of the Shadows: An Unfinished Sonnet-Sequence

26. I

*MS, holograph, initialed; TS¹, "Shadows"-A; TS², "Shadows"-B; TS³, "Shadows"-C; AME 1920

MS Alterations: 4 Echo] *w.o. erasure*
10 are thy] "y" *w.o. illeg.*

Variants: 2, 4, 6, 8, 10, 12 *[indentation]*] *no indentation* TS¹+
3 night-winds∧] ∼∧∼, TS¹+
3 hair∧] ∼, TS¹+

8 cry.] ∼; TS¹+
11 ringing,] ∼. TS¹+

Note: The MS, written on torn, blue-ruled, yellowish-brown pad paper (272 × 202 mm, 44 mm h. sp.), bears a canceled roman "I" in head space. Designation and placement as the first sonnet of the sequence derives from TS¹+. On the reverse side of the MS is a copy of Sonnet XVI [41, MS].

TS¹, on unwatermarked paper (103 × 216 mm), carries a penciled "1." in the upper left corner. "Out of the Shadows | An Unfinished Sonnet-Sequence" is typed at head, TS²⁻³.

27. II

MS¹, holograph draft; *MS², holograph, initialed; TS¹, "Shadows"-A; TS², "Shadows"-B; TS³, "Shadows"-C; AME 1920

Emendation: 10 breath∧] MS¹, TS¹+; ∼, MS²

MS¹ Alterations: 2 happy] *w.o. erasure*
4 the] *w.o. possible erasure*
6 Nor cared to] *w.o. erasure*
6 the . . . eyes,] *w.o. erasure*
9 Was . . . chords] *w.o. erasure; line 9 follows two canceled lines,* "Smile on me, Sweet, and lightened is my load, | Touch but my hand and happy is my heart."
10 Of . . . wakened] *w.o. erasure*
11 O'er] *w.o. erasure*
11 tender-spoken] "de" *traced over in what appears to be purple ink*
13 bade] "a" *w.o. illeg.*
13 own—] *dash written above comma*

MS² Alterations: 1 thee] *w.o. erased word*
2 Slender] *w.o. illeg.*
2 thy] *w.o. erased word* "your"?
5 thee] *w.o. erased word, probably* "you"
6 thy] *w.o. erased* "your"
6 eyes] *upper loop of first* "e" *and first stroke of* "y" *appear to be traced over in purple ink*
10 breath] "t" *w.o. illeg.*
14 dark-eyed] *w.o. erasure*

Variants: 1, 5 thee] you MS¹

2, 4, 6, 8, 10, 12 [*indentation*]] *no indentation* TS¹+

2 Slender] So lithe MS¹

2, 6 thy] your MS¹

5 then,] ~‸ TS¹+

7 where and when] when and where TS¹ (*penciled underlining of* when *and of* where *suggests that phrase is meant to be corrected by reversal of the two words*)

11 tender-spoken] ~‸~ TS¹+

12 soul-passioned] ~‸~ TS¹+

13 own —] ~; TS²+ (*semicolon appears to be w.o. dash, black ink* TS²⁻³)

14 dark-eyed] golden MS¹

Note: MS¹, written on torn, blue-ruled, yellowish-brown pad paper (248 × 204 mm, 26 mm t. sp.), bears a "II" above the poem. On the reverse side of MS¹ there is a holograph text of what appears to be an early, rejected first sonnet of the "Out of the Shadows" sequence [64, MS]. MS², written on the front side of the first school-tablet leaf, bears a canceled "II." above the poem and the date "8–13–'18 " above Cotter's initials at foot. Designation as the second sonnet of the sequence derives from MS¹, TS¹+. On the reverse side of the MS² leaf is a canceled draft of what is evidently another sonnet [65, MS], tried and rejected for the first position in the sequence.

TS¹, on unwatermarked paper (279.5 × 216 mm), carries a penciled "2." to the left of the first line of the poem. On TS¹⁻³ Sonnet II occupies the upper portion of the page above typescript of Sonnet III [28, TS¹⁻³].

28. III

*MS, holograph, initialed; TS¹, "Shadows"-A; TS², "Shadows"-B; TS³, "Shadows"-C; AME 1920

Emendations: 1 love?‸"] TS¹+; ~ ?," MS

5 its] TS¹+; it's MS

MS Alterations: 1 cries] "s" *w.o. erasure*

2 ah] "h" *w.o. illeg.*

2 die,] "ie," *appears to be w.o. erasure*

2 die.] "di" *appears to be w.o. erasure*

3 Burdened] *w.o. erasure*

3 with love's satiety,] "h love's satiety," *w.o. illeg.*

5 Keep] *w.o. illeg.*

†5 it's] *w.o. illeg.*

5 give] "ve" *w.o. illeg.*

6 the] *w.o. erasure*

6 dross] "ss" *w.o. illeg.*

8 morn.] *period appears to be w.o. comma*

10 love's fire;] "e's fire" *w.o. illeg.; upper part of semicolon might be remnant of erased material*

14 bounty] *w.o. erasure; may be partly traced over in purple ink*

14 true?] *question mark w.o. erasure*

Variants: 1 "What (*no indentation*)] *indented one space* TS¹

1 me;] ∼, *or* ∼. *could be reading on* TS¹ (*penciled punctuation mark w.o. typed semicolon*); ∼, TS²+

2 Ah∧] ∼, TS¹+

2 say;] ∼, TS¹+

4 it,] ∼∧ TS¹+

4 sigh.] ∼, AME 1920

8 morn.] ∼, TS²+

Note: The MS is dated "8–13–'18" at foot above Cotter's initials. It is written on the front of the second leaf of the school tablet and bears a canceled "III" in head space. Designation and placement as the third sonnet of the sequence derives from TS¹+. On the back of the manuscript leaf is a copy of Sonnet IV [29, MS³].

TS¹ is on unwatermarked paper (279.5 × 216 mm) and carries a penciled "3." in the left margin opposite the first line. On TS¹⁻³, Sonnet III occupies the lower half of the page below typescript of Sonnet II [27, TS¹⁻³].

29. IV

MS¹, holograph draft, lines 1–8 only; MS², holograph draft, lines 9–14 only; *MS³, holograph, initialed; TS¹, "Shadows"-A; TS², "Shadows"-B; TS³, "Shadows"-C; AME 1920

Emendation: 8 poor.] MS¹, TS¹+; ∼, MS³

MS' Alterations: 1 Why . . . voice] *line follows canceled line,* "What shall I bring for my love's holiday?"

4 Blue-girt and] "ir", "nd" *w.o. illeg.*

4 each] "ea" *w.o. illeg.*

6 or glen . . . moor,] *w.o. erased words*

8 be the] "the" *w.o. erased word*

MS² Alterations: 10 give . . . trips —] *w.o. erased words; dash appears to be w.o. semicolon*

13 Laughter . . . fee,] *w.o. erased words*

14 Deep . . . treasure] *w.o. erased words; line 14 follows canceled beginning of line,* "Smile [?] [*illeg.*] Sweet [?],"

MS³ Alterations: 1 living] "living" *written on blue-ruled line just above, perhaps to clarify script on line* 1

7 each to] "a" *w.o. illeg.*

11 Song-burthened] "ong" *w.o. illeg.*

Variants: 2, 4, 6, 8, 10, 12 [*indentation*]] *no indentation* TS¹+

4 silvered] s{\i}levered AME 1920

5 though] tho MS¹

5 God-sent] ~ˏ~ TS¹⁻³

6 field,] ~ˏ MS¹, TS¹+

6 glen,] ~ˏ MS¹

7 softlyˏ] ~, TS¹+

11 wind-blown] dark brown MS²

12 lips,] ~. MS²

13 fee,] ~ˏ TS¹+

Note: MS¹, on blue-lined, yellowish-brown pad paper (252 × 200 mm, 48 mm h. sp.), gives only the first eight lines of the sonnet below a "IV". A penciled outline of a paper clip is in the upper left corner. On the reverse side of MS¹ is a copy of Sonnet V [30, MS¹]. Also on blue-ruled, yellowish-brown pad paper (252 × 200 mm, 48 mm h. sp.) and occupying the top half of the page, MS² gives only the last six lines of the sonnet below a "IV". A copy of the previously unpublished poem beginning "Never, never shall I clothe" [62, MS] is written on the lower half of the page. On the reverse side of MS² is a copy of "Love's Demesne" [56, MS¹]. MS³, on the back of the second school-tablet leaf, is dated "9–5–'18" above the initials "J.S.C. Jr." at the foot to the left. The same date and initials, mostly erased, appear in the lower right corner. The "IV." above the poem is canceled, and designation as the fourth sonnet derives from MS¹⁻², TS¹+. On the front of MS³ is a copy of Sonnet III [28, MS].

TS¹, on unwatermarked paper (279.5 × 216 mm), carries a penciled "4" to the left of the first lines of the poem. On TS¹⁻³, Sonnet IV appears above typescript of Sonnet V [30, TS¹⁻³].

30. V

MS¹, holograph; *MS², holograph, initialed; TS¹, "Shadows"-A; TS², "Shadows"-B; TS³, "Shadows"-C; AME 1920

MS¹ Alterations: 1 dwell,] *w.o. erasure*
2 peace] "ace" *w.o. illeg.*
2 bides the time,] *w.o. erasure*
3 boundless] *w.o. illeg.*
4 fairest moments] *w.o. erasure*
6 one] *top of* "e" *traced over in purple ink*
7 a] *probably w.o. erasure*
8 I stand] *w.o. erasure*
9 Send] "en" *and lower parts of* "S" *and* "d" *traced over in purple ink*
9 purging . . . love,] *w.o. erasure*
10 Suaging my] *w.o. erasure*
11 rove] "r" *w.o. illeg.*
12 the] *w.o. illeg.*
13 follows] *appears to be w.o. erasure*
13 amain —] *dash appears to be w.o. semicolon*
14 fleeting] "ing" *w.o. illeg.*

MS² Alterations: 5 weeping, . . . passing] *w.o. erasure*
6 after-glow] "ow" *w.o. illeg.*
7 a] *may be w.o. erasure*
7 brief] *w.o. illeg.*
10 my] "m" *w.o. illeg.*
10 consuming] "suming" *w.o. illeg.*
13 For] *w.o. erasure*

Variants: 2, 4, 6, 8, 10, 12 [*indentation*]] *no indentation* TS¹+
5 men, weeping, spend a] men∧ spend one fleeting, MS¹; men∧ weeping∧ spend a TS¹+
7 a] one MS¹

9 love,] *apparent comma at end of line 9 on* MS[1] *may be remnant of erased material;* ~‸ TS[1]+

10 Suaging] Suageing MS[1]

13 For] But MS[1]

Note: MS[1], written on blue-ruled, yellowish-brown pad paper (252 × 200 mm, 48 mm h. sp.), bears large "V" in head space. On reverse side of MS[1] is a copy of the first eight lines of Sonnet IV [29, MS[1]]. MS[2], on the front of the third leaf of school tablet, is dated "9–10–18." at foot above initials "J.S.C. Jr.", and a canceled "V" appears in the head space. Designation and placement as the fifth sonnet of the sequence derives from MS[1], TS[1]+. On the back of MS[2] is a copy of Sonnet VI [31, MS[2]].

TS[1], on unwatermarked paper (279.5 × 216 mm), bears a penciled "5" to the left of the first lines of the poem. On TS[1–3], Sonnet V appears below Sonnet IV [29, TS[1–3]].

31. VI

MS[1], holograph draft, initialed; *MS[2], holograph, initialed; TS[1], "Shadows"-A; TS[2], "Shadows"-B; TS[3], "Shadows"-C; AME 1920

Emendation: 4 tears,] MS[1], TS[1]+; ~. MS[2]

MS[1] Alterations: 2 Awaken memories] *apparent initial stroke of letter to follow* "Awaken" *springs from* "n", *just before apparent erasure between* "Awaken" *and* "memories"

3 Arouse] *w.o. erasure*

4 Becloud] *w.o. erasure*

4 flood the] *erasure between these words*

5 Soft . . . charm,] *follows canceled phrase on line above,* "Soft, soothing hands that"

5 ancient] *w.o. erasure*

6 love's roundelay,] *erasure between these words; what appears to be period between* "roundelay" *and the comma is probably remnant of erased material*

7 thy] *w.o. erasure*

8 day.] *period w.o. what appears to be erased dash*

10 dwells] "ll" *w.o. illeg.*

11 must] "us" *w.o. illeg.*

11 fate] "f" *w.o. what appears to be erased* "F"
12 my] *w.o. erasure*
12 age's] "a" *w.o. illeg.*
12 sable] "e" *w.o. erasure*

MS² Alteration: 7 slender] *w.o. erasure*

Variants: 2, 4, 6, 8, 10, 12 [*indentation*]] *no indentation* TS¹+
5 Soft,] ~∧ TS¹+
7 Firm,] ~∧ TS¹+
7 slender] langorous MS¹
8 Dark,] ~∧ TS¹+
8 day.] ~— TS¹+
11 merciless∧] ~, MS¹
12 gown.] ~, MS¹
13 Though] Tho MS¹
13 laid,] ~∧ TS¹+

Note: Written on blue-ruled, yellowish-brown pad paper (272 × 202 mm, 42 mm h. sp.), MS¹ carries a large "VI" above the poem. Below the poem the date "9–24–18" appears above the initials "J.S.C. Jr." On the reverse side of MS¹ is a copy of Sonnet VII [32, MS²]. MS², written on the back of the third leaf of the school tablet, carries the date "9–24–'18." at foot above initials "J.S.C. Jr." Above the poem is a canceled "VI". Designation and placement as the sixth sonnet of the sequence derives from MS¹, TS¹+. On the front of MS² leaf is a copy of Sonnet V [30, MS²].

TS¹, on unwatermarked paper (118 × 216 mm), bears a "6." penciled in the left margin. On TS²⁻³ Sonnet VI appears above Sonnet VII [32, TS²⁻³].

32. VII

MS¹, holograph draft; MS², holograph, initialed; *MS³, holograph, initialed; TS¹, "Shadows"-A; TS², "Shadows"-B; TS³, "Shadows"-C; AME 1920

MS¹ Alterations: †4 new-blown] *w.o. erasure*
†9 O,] *w.o. erasure*
14 gleams] *w.o. erasure*

MS² Alterations: 3 And press] *w.o. erasure*
3 purpled] *w.o. erasure*
4 cheeks] "k" *w.o. what may have been* "p"
6 And peacefully] *w.o. erasure*
7 Deep in] *w.o. illeg.*
8 Casting] *w.o. erasure*

Variants: 1 come and go] on your face MS¹; come & go MS²
2, 4, 6, 8, 10, 12 [*indentation*]] *no indentation* TS¹+
2 In . . . face,] Play hide and seek about your loveliness; MS¹
3 press . . . glow] on your crimson lips there blooms the grace MS¹
4 crimson . . . grace] new-blown roses, 'mid the comeliness MS¹
5 They . . . skies,] Of blushing dawn upon the eastern skies. MS¹; They
    kiss your lips as night enwraps the skies, MS²
6 And peacefully they] The lilting shadows MS¹
6 and] & MS²
9 O∧ then,] ∼, ∼∧ MS¹
10 by] with MS¹
11 earth] earth's MS¹, TS¹+
12 live] dwell MS¹
12 beguile] bequile TS¹

Note: MS¹, written on blue-ruled, yellowish-brown pad paper (272 ×
202 mm, 43.5 mm h. sp.), carries a "VII." centered in the head space and
the date "9–25–'18." at foot. The entire text of the poem on MS¹ is crossed
out in pencil with three large exes. MS², also on blue-ruled, yellowish-
brown pad paper (272 × 202 mm), bears a "VII" above the poem and the
date "9–26,–'18." above the initials "J.S.C. Jr." at foot. On the reverse side
of MS² is a copy of Sonnet VI [31, MS¹]. Written on the front of the fourth
school-tablet leaf, MS³ bears a canceled "VII" above the poem and the
date "9–25–'18" above the initials "J.S.C. Jr." below. (The dating of MS³
appears to reflect Cotter's general tendency to retain dates of early drafts
when dating later copies. Thus, the later date on MS² is unusual.) Desig-
nation as the seventh sonnet derives from MS¹⁻², TS¹+. On the reverse
side of the manuscript leaf is a copy of Sonnet VIII [33, MS²].
    On unwatermarked paper (279.5 × 216 mm), TS¹ carries "7." to the left
above the poem that occupies the upper part of the page above typescript
of Sonnet VIII [33, TS¹]. Sonnet VII is below VI [31, TS²⁻³] on TS²⁻³.

33. VIII

MS¹, holograph draft, initialed; *MS², holograph, initialed; TS¹, "Shadows"-A; TS², "Shadows"-B; TS³, "Shadows"-C; AME 1920

Emendation: 13 passion‸] ~, MS²+

MS¹ Alterations: 2 nebulous] "e" *w.o. illeg.*
5 Garbed . . . skies,] *follows canceled line,* "Out from the [*illeg.*]"; *the comma appears to be altered from a period*
5 vaulted] *w.o. erasure*
7 When] *much of upper loop of* "h" *may be traced over in purple ink*
8 And] *upper portion of* "n" *appears to be reinforced in purple ink over erasure*
9 from] *w.o. erasure*
9 ages over hungered] *w.o. erasure*
11 Searing] *w.o. illeg.*

MS² Alterations: 3 God] *penciled line above* "G" *of unknown significance*
6 way,] *mark following comma of unknown significance, looks almost like second comma*
14 thee] *pencil marks above* "t" *of unknown significance*

Variants: 1 earth‸ . . . desire‸‸] ~, . . . ~ „ TS¹ (*two commas at end of line added in pencil*); ~, . . . ~, TS²+
2, 4, 6, 8, 10, 12 [*indentation*]] *no indentation* TS¹+
4 And . . . charm.] And . . . charm ⟨ ⟩MS¹ (*punctuation mark at end of line removed by tear*)
7 Eden-wise,] ~-~‸ MS¹
11 scrolls,] ~. TS¹⁻³
13 Crowned with the years‸] Ancient of days, MS¹

Note: MS¹ is on torn, blue-ruled, yellowish-brown pad paper (272 × 201.5 mm, 44 mm h. sp.) and bears an "VIII" above the text of the poem. The date "10–1–'18" appears in the lower left corner above initials "J.S.C. Jr." On the reverse side of MS¹ is a copy of Sonnet IX [34, MS¹]. On the back of the fourth leaf of the school tablet, MS² carries the date "10–1–'18" at foot above initials "J.S.C. Jr." The "VIII" above the poem is canceled, and designation as the eighth sonnet stems from MS¹, TS¹+. On the front of the manuscript leaf is a copy of Sonnet VII [32, MS³].

TS¹, on unwatermarked paper (279.5 × 216 mm), carries a penciled "8" to the left just above the poem, which is typed below typescript of Sonnet VII [32, TS¹]. On TS²⁻³ Sonnet VIII appears above Sonnet IX [34, TS²⁻³].

34. IX

MS¹, holograph draft; *MS², holograph, initialed; TS¹, "Shadows"-A; TS², "Shadows"-B; TS³, "Shadows"-C; AME 1920

Emendation: 13 gone, but . . . renews₍ₐ₎] TS¹+; ∼ₐ∼ . . . ∼ₐ MS¹; ∼ₐ∼ . . . ∼, MS²

MS¹ Alterations: †3 the mystic] "e", "mystic" *w.o. erasure*
4 olden wraiths] *w.o. erasure*
5 forgotten] *w.o. erased word*
†6 spent . . . years;] *w.o. erased words*
10 Keeping . . . arms,] *follows two canceled lines,* "And [*illeg.*] me thy warrior, | And th[*illeg.*] of God's [*illeg.*] light,"

MS² Alterations: 3 magic] "agic" *w.o. erasure*
11 battle] "battle" *interlined above the same, undeleted word* "battle", *probably to clarify handwriting*
12 Thy] "y" *w.o.* "e"

Variants: 2, 4, 6, 8, 10, 12 [*indentation*]] *no indentation* TS¹+
3 breathe] breath (*pencil underlined*) TS¹ (*penciled underlining, suggesting need for correction*)
3 magic] mystic MS¹
4 grace!] ∼. MS¹
5 dim,] ∼ₐ TS¹+
6 years,] ∼; MS¹
8 fears.] ∼, MS¹
9 pledgéd] pledged TS¹+
12 made easeful] shone clear midst MS¹
12 alarms.] ∼, TS²+

Note: On torn, blue-ruled, yellowish-brown pad paper (272 × 201.5 mm), MS¹ bears a "IX" at head. Below the poem, the word "Phrases." is written above a horizontal penciled line drawn across the page. Below the line, Cotter wrote, "The pleasing after-glow of memory .1 | The habitation of eternal joys. 2". On the reverse side of MS¹ is a copy of Sonnet VIII [33,

MS¹]. MS² is written on the front of the fifth school-tablet leaf and bears the date "10–11–'18" in the lower left corner, above the initials "J.S.C. Jr." At head is a canceled "IX". Designation as the ninth sonnet derives from MS¹, TS¹+. On the back of the manuscript leaf is a holograph copy of Sonnet X [35, MS].

TS¹, on unwatermarked paper (279.5 × 216 mm), carries a penciled "9" to the left just above the poem, which appears above typescript of Sonnet X [35, TS¹]. The pencil-canceled partial line "Passion of fire that sears my burning" is typed at head of the verso of TS¹ on wine-colored ribbon. On TS²⁻³, Sonnet IX is on the lower half of the page, below Sonnet VIII [33, TS²⁻³].

35. X

*MS, holograph, initialed; TS¹, "Shadows"-A; TS², "Shadows"-B; TS³, "Shadows"-C; AME 1920

Emendations: 10 Give] TS¹+; Gives MS
14 conqueror's] AME 1920; conquerer's MS, TS¹⁻³

MS Alterations: 6 Pensive] "e" *w.o.* "e"?
6 beneath . . . sky,] *w.o. erased words*
7 fires . . . rhyme,] *w.o. erased words*
8 words to clothe the old-time cry.] *partly erased underlining beginning at mid-point below* "words", *probably to mark the passage for revision; phrase* "to clothe the old-time cry." *w.o. erased words; beneath* "ot" *of* "clothe" *but above the long, partly erased underlining, is a short, dark line of unknown significance*
†10 Gives . . . desire,] *line w.o. erased words*

Variants: 1 hour,] ~∧ TS¹+
2, 4, 6, 8, 10, 12 [*indentation*]] *no indentation* TS¹+
5 time,] ~∧ TS¹+
9 years,] ~∧ TS¹+
14 wield] to wield TS¹+

Note: The MS, written on the back of the fifth school-tablet leaf, is dated "10–11–'18." above initials "J.S.C. Jr." in the lower left corner. A canceled "X" appears above the poem. Position and designation as the tenth sonnet derives from TS¹+. On the front of the manuscript leaf is a copy of Sonnet IX [34, MS²].

TS¹, on unwatermarked paper (279.5 × 216 mm), bears a penciled "10" to the left of the first line of the poem, which occupies the lower half of the page below typescript of Sonnet IX [34, TS¹]. See Apparatus note to Sonnet IX regarding the canceled line typed on the verso of TS¹. On TS²⁻³, Sonnet X appears above typescript of Sonnet XI [36, TS²⁻³].

36. XI

*MS, holograph, initialed; TS¹, "Shadows"-A; TS², "Shadows"-B; TS³, "Shadows"-C; AME 1920

Emendations: 1 deignst] TS¹+; deigns't MS
5 hair₍ₐ₎] TS¹+; ~, MS
8 singest.] TS¹+; ~₍ₐ₎ MS

MS Alterations: 4 beguilest] "b" *w.o. illeg.*
7 a-quiver] "q" *and* "er" *w.o. illeg.*
10 o'er] "er" *w.o. illeg.*
11 I] *w.o. erasure*

Variants: 2, 4, 6, 8, 10, 12 *[indentation]] no indentation* TS¹+
5 shadows,] ~₍ₐ₎ TS¹+
7 is₍ₐ₎a-quiver] ~-~-~TS¹+
9 song₍ₐ₎] ~, TS¹+
9 strain,] ~₍ₐ₎ TS¹+
10 holdest;] ~, TS¹+

Note: The MS, written on the front of the sixth school-tablet leaf, is dated "10–17–'18." above initials "J.S.C. Jr." in the lower left corner. A canceled "XI." appears above the poem. Designation as the eleventh sonnet derives from TS¹+. On the back of the manuscript leaf is a copy of Sonnet XII [37, MS].

On unwatermarked paper (279 × 216 mm), TS¹ carries a penciled "11" to the left of the first line of the poem, which appears above typescript of Sonnet XII [37, TS¹]. See Apparatus note to Sonnet XII regarding slip attached at the bottom of TS¹. On TS²⁻³, Sonnet XI appears below typescript of Sonnet X [35, TS²⁻³].

37. XII

*MS, holograph, initialed; TS¹, "Shadows"-A; TS², "Shadows"-B; TS³, "Shadows"-C; AME 1920

Emendation: 12 crown.$_\wedge$] TS¹+; ~,, MS

MS Alterations: 5 stately] "a" *w.o. illeg.*
8 eery] *pencil mark below first* "e" *of unknown significance*
11 stars] "tars" *w.o. illeg.*
†12 Jewels . . . crown,,] *w.o. erased words; a short penciled line below* "Jewels" *is of unknown significance*

Variants: 1 dusk$_\wedge$] ~, TS¹, AME 1920
1 threads$_\wedge$] ~, TS¹+
2, 4, 6, 8, 10, 12 [*indentation*]] *no indentation* TS¹+
2 earth, a-fevered,] ~$_\wedge$ ~-~$_\wedge$ TS¹+
3 $_\wedge$round] '~ TS¹+
4 hour.] ~, AME 1920
5 Night-winds] ~$_\wedge$~ TS¹+
6 sky;] ~$_\wedge$ TS¹⁻³; ~. AME 1920
7 Night-birds] ~$_\wedge$~ TS¹+
7 vines,] ~. TS¹⁻³; ~$_\wedge$ AME 1920
8 an eery] and every AME 1920
8 cry.] ~, TS²+
10 dusk$_\wedge$] ~, TS¹⁻³
11 thee,] ~$_\wedge$ TS¹+

Note: On the back of the sixth school-tablet leaf, MS is dated "10–29–'18." above the initials "J.S.C. Jr." in the lower left corner. A canceled "XII." is above the poem; designation as the twelfth sonnet derives from TS¹+. On the front of the manuscript leaf is a copy of Sonnet XI [36, MS].

TS¹, on unwatermarked paper (279 × 216 mm), bears a penciled "12." to the left of the first line of the poem, which is typed below Sonnet XI [36, TS¹]. Attached with a straight pin at the foot is a slip of paper (35 irreg. × 198 mm) on which line 7, Sonnet XII, omitted from typescript, is penciled in what is probably Cotter Sr.'s hand. A penciled line is drawn from the slip to the place of the omitted line on typescript. On TS²⁻³, Sonnet XII appears above typescript of XIII [38, TS²⁻³].

38. XIII

*MS, holograph; TS¹, "Shadows"-A; TS², "Shadows"-B; TS³, "Shadows"-C; AME 1920

Emendation: 12 lees.] TS¹+; lee's/.. MS

MS Alterations: 1 passing] "a" *w.o. illeg.*
6 Of] "O" *w.o.* "o"
6 foam-crest oceans and the] *w.o. erased words; line below "the" may have been associated with erased material*
6 wood] "ood" *w.o. erasure*
8 minds . . . dark] *w.o. erased words; partially erased underlining from "minds" to end of line 8 may have marked passage for revision*
9 blue-girt] "girt" *w.o. illeg.*
10 bound] "n" *w.o. illeg.*
10 in . . . breeze,] *w.o. erased words*
11 But . . . melody,] *w.o. erased words*
†12 quaff thy spirits-passioned lee's/..] *w.o. erasure; one of the periods may be remnant of erased material*

Variants: 2, 4, 6, 8, 10, 12 [*indentation*]] *no indentation* TS¹+
6 tangled] angled AME 1920
8 deep-nurtured] ∼ˌ∼ TS¹+
11 melody,] ∼ˌ TS¹+
12 spirits-passioned] spirit'sˌpassioned TS¹+

Note: The MS is written on the front of the seventh leaf of the school tablet and bears a canceled "XIII" in the head space. Position and designation as the thirteenth sonnet derives from TS¹+. A copy of Sonnet XIV [39, MS] is on the back of the manuscript leaf.

TS¹, on unwatermarked paper (279.5 × 216 mm), carries a penciled "13." to the left of the first lines of the poem. On TS¹, Sonnet XIII appears above a typescript of Sonnet XIV [39, TS¹]; on TS²⁻³, Sonnet XIII is typed below Sonnet XII [37, TS²⁻³].

39. XIV

*MS, holograph, initialed; TS¹, "Shadows"-A; TS², "Shadows"-B; TS³, "Shadows"-C; AME 1920

MS Alterations: 3 when] "en" *w.o. illeg.*
9 The] "e" *w.o. erasure*
10 love's . . . breath] *w.o. erased words*
11 bourgeouny] *w.o. erasure*
12 my] *may be w.o. erasure*
12 heaven's star-gold wreath.] *w.o. erased words*
13 tear-swept] *diagonal pencil mark between "s" and "w", significance unclear*

Variants: 2, 4, 6, 8, 10, 12 [*indentation*]] *no indentation* TS¹+
3 vision,] ∼‸ TS¹+
7 despair,] ∼‸ TS¹+
13 moan,] ∼. AME 1920
14 ‸mid] '∼ TS¹+

Note: The MS, written on the back of the seventh school-tablet leaf, is dated "11–1–'18." at foot above the initials "J.S.C. Jr." A canceled "XIV" is at head, and designation of the poem as the fourteenth sonnet derives from TS¹+. On the front of the leaf there is a copy of Sonnet XIII [38, MS].

On unwatermarked paper (279.5 × 216 mm), TS¹ bears a penciled "14." to the left of the first line of the poem. On TS¹, Sonnet XIV appears below Sonnet XIII [38, TS¹] and above Sonnet XV [40, TS²⁻³] on TS²⁻³.

40. XV

MS¹, holograph; *MS², holograph; TS¹, "Shadows"-A; TS², "Shadows"-B; TS³, "Shadows"-C; AME 1920

MS¹ Alterations: 1 by,] *w.o. erased word; the comma follows erased material*
3 faintly] *w.o. erased word*
3 sky,] *w.o. erased word*
4 And] *w.o. erased word*
4 slowly with] *w.o. erasure*
12 These] "T" *w.o. illeg.*

MS² Alteration: 10 beck] "b" *w.o. illeg.*

Variants: 2, 4, 6, 8, 10, 12 [*indentation*]] *no indentation* TS¹+
4 night.] ∼; TS¹+
5 sun,] ∼‸ MS¹
5 hidden‸] ∼, MS¹, TS¹+

10 Youth!] ∼, MS¹; youth! TS¹+
12 truth!] ∼. MS¹
13 shall] will MS¹
13 Love] love TS¹+

Note: MS¹ is on white, wove paper (280.5 × 215.5 mm) watermarked OLD DEERFIELD BOND. The date "11–9–'18" is written above initials "J.S.C. Jr." below the poem. The "XV" above the poem appears to be written over a previous numeral, perhaps "XIV". On the reverse side of MS¹ is a typed letter addressed to "Mr. Joseph S. Cotter Jr, ‖ 2306 Magazine Street, ‖ Louisville, Ky." below letterhead of "The Kny-Scheerer Corporation | SURGICAL AND ELECTRO-MEDICAL INSTRUMENTS | HOSPITAL AND SANITARIUM SUPPLIES | SCIENTIFIC APPARATUS ‖ 404–410 West 27th Street ‖ New York". The letter, dated "October 24th, 1918.", relates that the corporation cannot supply the "Discreet Pocket Sputum Cup" that Cotter had ordered "October 19th" and asks permission to substitute a different "style flask". The letter is signed "Betty" below the typed name of the corporation. MS², which bears no numeral, is written on the front of the eighth school-tablet leaf. Designation of the poem as the fifteenth sonnet derives from MS¹, TS¹+. On the back of the manuscript leaf is a copy of Sonnet XVII [42, MS²].

TS¹, on unwatermarked paper (279.5 × 215.5 mm), bears a "15" penciled in the left margin. Below Sonnet XV on TS¹ is typescript of Sonnet XVII [42, TS¹]. A penciled "16" is in the space between the two sonnets. On TS²⁻³, Sonnet XV appears below typescript of Sonnet XIV [39, TS²⁻³].

41. XVI

*MS, holograph, initialed; TS¹, "Shadows"-A; TS², "Shadows"-B; TS³, "Shadows"-C; AME 1920

Emendations: 6 wreath,] TS¹ (*comma handwritten over erasure*), TS³+; ∼; MS; ∼∧ TS²
7 Heart's∧passion,] TS¹+; Hearts-passion∧ MS
8 Heart's∧hope,] TS¹+; Hearts-hope∧ MS

MS Alterations: 3 labour] "l" *w.o. illeg.*
4 womb] "womb" *interlined above the same uncanceled word,* "womb"
5 band] "b" *w.o. illeg.*

†7 Hearts-passion] "s-" *w.o. erasure*
7 breath] "b" *w.o. illeg.*
14 murmurs] *initial* "m" *w.o. illeg.*

Variants: 2, 4, 6, 8, 10, 12 [*indentation*]] *no indentation* TS¹+
6 Sorrow] Sorow AME 1920
7 love's] love!s TS¹
8 hand;] ~, TS¹ (*comma appears to be penciled over typed semicolon*)
10 ∧ Mid] '~ TS²+
14 th'] the TS²+

Note: The MS is on blue-ruled, yellowish-brown pad paper (272 × 202 mm). A tear at the top of the MS has removed part of the canceled "XVI." above the poem. Designation and placement as the sixteenth sonnet derives from TS¹+. At foot are initials "JS.C Jr." above the date "11–13–'18." On the reverse side of MS is a copy of Sonnet I [26, MS].

A penciled "16." appears to the left of the first line of the poem on TS¹, which is typed on unwatermarked paper (177 × 216 mm). On TS²⁻³, Sonnet XVI occupies top half of page, above typescript of Sonnet XVII [42, TS²⁻³].

42. XVII

MS¹, holograph draft, initialed; *MS², holograph; TS¹, "Shadows"-A; TS², "Shadows"-B; TS³, "Shadows"-C; AME 1920

MS¹ Alterations: 1 is] *w.o. erased word*
1 bright hope] *w.o. erased words*
1 terrors] "s" *in darker, heavier pencil, appears added after writing of* "terror"
2 earthly . . . poor] *w.o. erased words*
3 errors] "s" *appears added later, as with* "s" *of* "terrors", *line* 1
4 bid me shun] *w.o. erased words*
5 my] *w.o. erased word*
7 frigid] *second* "i" *w.o. illeg.*
8 thy] *w.o. erased word, perhaps* "your"
10 Where . . . measures] *w.o. erased words*
11 my] *w.o. erased word*
12 stand halting] *erasure between these words*
12 dead] "ea" *and lower part of second* "d" *traced over in purple ink; erased*

word follows
14 Only that] *w.o. erased words*
14 lone] "ne" *written with much heavier pressure over illeg.*

MS² Alteration: 1 or] *w.o. illeg.*

Variants: 1 terrors,∧] ∼,, MS¹
2, 4, 6, 8, 10, 12 [*indentation*]] *no indentation* TS¹+
3 errors∧∧] ∼,, MS¹
4 easy,] ∼∧ TS¹+
9 dim,] ∼∧ TS¹+
9 earth∧] ∼, MS¹
10 sped,] ∼; MS¹
12 dead.] ∼∧ MS¹

Note: MS¹ is on a light blue unwatermarked half sheet (139 × 214 mm). The words "last. one." are written in what appears to be Cotter's hand at head. No other notation appears above the text of the poem. At foot are initials "J.S.C. Jr." above the date "11–21–'18." On the reverse side of MS¹ is a printed *Crisis* magazine form for submission of names of potential subscribers. The form is blank. MS², written on the back of the eighth leaf of the school tablet, bears no numeral, initials, or date. Designation of the poem as the seventeenth sonnet derives from TS¹+. Two accidentally drawn wavy ink lines extend across lines 4–10 of the poem on MS². On the front of the leaf is a copy of Sonnet XV [40, MS²].

TS¹, on unwatermarked paper (279.5 × 215.5 mm), bears a penciled "17" to the left of the first line of the poem, which is typed below typescript of Sonnet XV [40, TS¹]. A "16" is written in pencil in the space between sonnets. On TS²⁻³, Sonnet XVII appears below typescript of Sonnet XVI [41, TS²⁻³].

43. XVIII

*MS, holograph; TS¹, "Shadows"-A; TS², "Shadows"-B; TS³, "Shadows"-C; AME 1920

MS Alterations: 2 smiles] "es" *w.o. illeg.*
5 And all] "nd all" *w.o. erasure*
6 dreams] "s" *w.o. illeg.*
6 are] *w.o. illeg.*

10 hand in our hand,] *wavy underlining below these words is of unclear signifi-
cance*
12 Hallowed] "wed" *w.o. illeg.*

Variants: 2, 4, 6, 8, 10, 12 [*indentation*]] *no indentation* TS¹+
7 tomorrow] to-morrow TS¹+
10 Hope] hope TS¹+
10 treks] treaks TS²⁻³
11 belief,] ∼. TS¹+

Note: The MS is written on the front of the ninth leaf of the school tablet;
it bears no numeral. Designation as the eighteenth sonnet derives from
TS¹+.

TS¹, on unwatermarked paper (95 irreg. × 216 mm), bears a penciled
"18." in the left margin. On TS²⁻³, Sonnet XVIII is typed above typescript
of Sonnet XIX [44, TS²⁻³].

44. XIX

MS¹, holograph draft; *MS², holograph; TS¹, "Shadows"-A; TS², "Shad-
ows"-B; TS³, "Shadows"-C; AME 1920

MS¹ Alterations: 4 lone] *preceded by canceled* "bright"
7 there I heard] *interlined above canceled* "lo! it was"
8 thy] *w.o. illeg. word*
9 my] *w.o.* "thy"
9 pulsing] "s" *w.o. illeg.*
10 side —] *dash w.o. semicolon*
†11 He . . . mine] *line follows canceled line* "And lo! I felt this wasted form of
mine — "
12 and then] "and" *w.o.* "And"?
12 and cried] "and" *possibly squeezed in later and w.o. illeg.*
13 the] *mark on* "t" *may be faded purple ink*

MS² Alteration: 9 draws] *w.o. in heavier hand what may be the same word,*
"draws"

Variants: 2, 4, 6, 8, 10, 12 [*indentation*]] *no indentation* TS¹+
2 and eyes] and eye TS¹+

4 lone star] lonestar TS [1-3]
4 Bethlehem's] Bethelem's MS [1]
5 face$_\wedge$] ~, MS [1]
7 spoke,] ~$_\wedge$ TS [1]+
11 I saw] He bore MS [1]
11 beauty,] ~$_\wedge$ MS [1]
11 mine,] ~$_\wedge$ MS [1]
13 took the child] quickly drew MS [1]
13 me,] ~$_\wedge$ MS [1], AME 1920
14 That never was, nor is, nor e'er] The child that never was and ne'er MS [1]

Note: MS [1] is written on the back of the white, stiff cover of a writing tablet (263 × 196.5 mm). At foot of MS [1] Cotter wrote, "Another version of 13 & 14 | God heard the cry and took the child from me, | That never was, nor is, nor e'er shall be". The word "took" is written above canceled "drew" in this revised version of line 13. (See illustration.) The "SIMON PURE | LINEN | Writing Tablet" trademark logo is printed on the reverse side of MS [1]. MS [2], on blue-ruled, yellowish-brown pad paper (263 irreg. × 203.5 mm, 26 mm h. sp. to perforation), bears no numeral (see illustration), and designation of the poem as the nineteenth sonnet stems from TS [1]+.

TS [1], on unwatermarked paper (279 × 216 mm), carries a penciled "19" in the upper left margin. On TS [2-3], Sonnet XIX appears below typescript of Sonnet XVIII [43, TS [2-3]].

Poems

45. IMMORTALITY

MS [1], holograph; *MS [2], holograph, signed; TS [1], "Shadows"-A; TS [2], "Shadows"-B; TS [3], "Shadows"-C; AME 1921

MS [2] Alterations: 1 trenchant] "enchant" *w.o. erasure*
2 future's] "re's" *w.o. erasure*
2 ken] *small check mark below word is of unclear significance*

Variants: 2, 4 [*no indentation*]] *marked to indent three spaces* TS [1]; *indented three spaces* TS [2-3]; *indented two spaces* AME 1921
2 future's] future!s TS [1]

2 ken‸] Ken‸ MS¹; ken— AME 1921
3 hold—] ~‸ TS¹+

Note: MS¹, written above a holograph copy of "Looking at a Portrait" [49, MS¹] on blue-ruled, yellowish-brown pad paper (273 × 201.5 mm, 53 mm h. sp.), is dated "May 5, 1918". A period follows the title. MS², also dated "May 5, 1918.", is written above a holograph copy of "A Woman at Her Husband's Grave" [46, MS³] on the back of the third ring-binder leaf. On the front of the leaf is a holograph copy of "The Mulatto to His Critics" [2, MS].

TS¹, on unwatermarked paper (279.5 × 215 mm), carries the page number "1" penciled in the upper left corner. On TS¹⁻³, "Immortality" is at the top of the page above "A Woman at Her Husband's Grave" [46, TS¹⁻³], "Night Winds" [47, TS¹⁻³], and "I Shall Not Die" [48, MS, TS¹⁻²].

46. A WOMAN AT HER HUSBAND'S GRAVE

MS¹, holograph draft, initialed; MS², holograph, signed; *MS³, holograph, signed; TS¹, "Shadows"-A; TS², "Shadows"-B; TS³, "Shadows"-C; AME 1921

Emendation: 5 Grieve] MS¹⁻², TS¹+; Greive MS³

MS¹ Alterations: †2 not, . . . me,] *commas appear to have been added later in heavier hand*
3 Sorrowing bow,] *w.o. erased words with heavier pressure, as with commas, line 2*
†4 me,] *comma appears added in heavier hand*
6 'Tis . . . gone] *follows what appear to be five canceled lines,* "Ah [?] [illeg.] | But [illeg.] were pain | To me who [illeg.] | A lover [illeg.] | Rest to his spirit!"

MS² Alteration: 8 husband] *preceded by canceled word,* "lover"?

MS³ Alteration: †5 Greive] *small penciled check mark below word, probably to mark spelling error*

Variants: 2 cannot‸] *reading on* MS¹ *could be* can not, *or* cannot,
2 me‸] ~, MS¹⁻²
4 me‸] ~, MS¹

7 heart-break] ∼∧∼ TS[1]+
7 over,] ∼; MS[1–2]
9 lover.] ∼∧ MS[2]

Note: MS[1], written vertically on the back of a letter within the middle column of three formed by the leaf's two horizontal folds, is titled "A Woman At Husband's Grave." A row of five short lines sets off title from text. The white, wove paper (279.5 × 215.5 mm) is watermarked with a seal framing the initials EPH. MS[1] is dated "May 24, 1918" and initialed "J.S.C. Jr." below a horizontal pencil line at foot. The form letter on the reverse side is dated "April 29, 1918." below the letterhead of "American Intercollegiate Football Rules Committee ‖ (Central Board on Officials)" . . . . "JAS. A. BABBITT, CHAIRMAN | HAVERFORD COLLEGE . . . | . . . . | H. W. TAYLOR, SEC'Y | 1901 CHESTNUT STREET, PHILADELPHIA". With the salutation "My dear Sir:" the letter requests information to assist in the compilation of a "list of men who will | be available as football officials during the season of 1918." It is signed "H.W. Taylor," "Secretary.", under the typed name "WALTER CAMP, Acting Chairman."

MS[2], written on blue-lined, yellowish-brown pad paper (272 × 201.5 mm, 53 mm h. sp.) is dated "5–24–'18" and signed at foot. The title on MS[2–3] is written "A Woman at Her Husband's Grave." Written below a copy of "Immortality" [45, MS[2]] on the back of the third ring-binder leaf, MS[3] carries the date "May 24, 1918", Cotter's signature, and the notation "Copy" at foot. On the front of the leaf is a copy of "The Mulatto to His Critics" [2, MS].

On unwatermarked paper (279.5 × 215 mm), TS[1] bears a penciled page number "1" in the upper left corner. On TS[1–3], "A Woman at Her Husband's Grave" is in second position, below "Immortality" [45, TS[1–3]] and above "Night Winds" [47, TS[1–3]] and "I Shall Not Die" [48, MS, TS[1–2]].

47. NIGHT WINDS

MS[1], holograph draft, signed; *MS[2], holograph, signed; TS[1], "Shadows"-A; TS[2], "Shadows"-B; TS[3], "Shadows"-C; AME 1921

MS[1] Alterations: 2 with] *w.o. illeg.*
5 moon] *second "o" may be w.o. illeg.; small penciled check mark above second "o" may indicate point for correction*

5 whisper to] *precedes possible erased comma*

MS² Alteration: 8 what] "hat" *w.o. erasure*

Variants: 1 in] is in TS¹+
2 stars‿] ~, MS¹
3 dreamy,] ~‿ MS¹, TS¹+
5 to,] ~‿ MS¹
6 kiss,] ~‿ MS¹
6 ‿mid] '~ TS²+
7 listening,] ~‿ MS¹; lightening, AME 1921

Note: MS¹, dated "June 19, 1918", is on blue-ruled, yellowish-brown pad paper (272 × 201.5 mm, 53 mm h. sp.). This draft carries no title. Below the poem there is a canceled phrase in Cotter's hand: "A full- [*illeg.*] moon of a yester-night". On the reverse side of MS¹ is a holograph copy of the previously unpublished poem beginning "Full well he knew the gall . . ." [61, MS]. MS², on the back of the fifth ring-binder leaf, is dated "June 19, 1918", and "Copy" is written below Cotter's signature at foot. On the front of the leaf is a copy of "Then I Would Love You" [8, MS].

    TS¹ is on unwatermarked paper (279.5 × 215 mm) and carries the penciled page number "1" in the upper left corner. On TS¹⁻³, "Night Winds" is in third position, typed below "Immortality" [45, TS¹⁻³] and "A Woman at Her Husband's Grave" [46, TS¹⁻³] and above "I Shall Not Die" [48, MS, TS¹⁻²].

48. I SHALL NOT DIE

*MS, "Shadows"-A; TS¹, "Shadows"-B; TS², "Shadows"-C; AME 1921

MS Alterations: 3 constellation] *first* "t" *inserted later*
4 faith-embraced] "f" *w.o. what is probably* "F"
4 soul] "s" *w.o. what is probably erased* "S"; "ul" *w.o. illeg. erased letters*

Variants: 2, 3 [*indented one space*]] *indented three spaces* TS¹⁻²

Note: MS, on unwatermarked paper (279.5 × 215 mm) with penciled page number "1" in the upper left corner, is written in pencil in what is probably the hand of Cotter Sr. and bears curved lines to the left of the poem to indicate desired indentations. MS title is written "I Shall Not Die.", with "N" following false start of "n". The first three lines of the poem appear to be written over erased portions of the same three lines, probably to establish desired spacing and indentations. MS is written at the bottom of the page, below typescripts of "Immortality" [45, TS¹], "A Woman at Her Husband's Grave" [46, TS¹], and "Night Winds" [47, TS¹]. "I Shall Not Die" is typed below the same three poems on TS¹⁻².

49. LOOKING AT A PORTRAIT

MS¹, holograph draft, initialed; MS², holograph, signed; *MS³, holograph, signed; TS¹, "Shadows"-A; TS², "Shadows"-B; TS³, "Shadows"-C; AME 1921

MS¹ Alterations: 1 why] "y" *w.o. illeg.*
1 these,] *comma appears to be w.o. erasure*
†4 Are . . . gleaming] *w.o. erasure*
†4 passion's] *w.o. erasure; two short penciled lines below "passion's" are of unknown significance*
7 breeze,] *dot following the comma looks almost like a period*
8 a] *follows canceled "as"*
9 each] *w.o. erasure*
11–12 O . . . please] *the greater part of these lines appears to be w.o. erased words, including erased signature of author which spans the two lines to the right*
13 weak] *w.o. erasure*
13 heart,] *w.o. lower loop of "J" of author's erased signature*
13 in their] *w.o. erasure*
15 O . . . these?] *appears to be w.o. remnant of earlier pencil draft*

MS² Alterations: 10 there] "re" *w.o. illeg.*
12 crush] "r" *w.o. illeg.*
14 Bring a glow of red to] "Bring" *interlined above uncanceled "Weave";* "to" *interlined above uncanceled "in"*

MS³ Alterations: 9 soul-cry] *hyphen appears to be added or reinforced later*
9 lave] *small check mark below word is of unclear significance*
11 O] *appears to be partly traced over in purple ink*
12 crumple] "e" *w.o. illeg.*
15 why] "y" *w.o. illeg.*

Variants: 1 O (*no indentation*)] *indented one space* TS¹
1, 5 O∧] ~, MS¹

3 So∧] That, MS¹

3 morning, so] morning∧ and MS¹

3 night,] night ⟨ ⟩ MS¹ (*because of tear, punctuation uncertain*); *comma very faint and not certain on* MS²; ~ ∧ TS¹+

4 Dancing] Are dancing MS¹

4 passioned delight] passion's light MS¹

6, 10, 11, 15 O∧] ~, MS¹; Oh∧ AME 1921

7 Caressed by] That laugh with MS¹; Caressed with MS²

7 breeze] breexe TS¹

14 Bring a glow of red to] Weave a glow of red in MS¹

15 ∧O] –~ TS¹

Note: MS¹, dated "May 14, 1918" in the right margin, is written below a copy of "Immortality" [45, MS¹] on blue-ruled, yellowish-brown pad paper (273 × 201.5 mm, 53 mm h. sp.). MS¹ title is written "Looking At A Portrait", with first "A" altered from "a" and second "A" written over an illegible letter. In the space between the second and third stanzas the erased date "May [*illeg.*] 1918" and Cotter's erased signature are partly legible, suggesting that the poem originally concluded with the second stanza. In the lower right corner of MS¹ the initials "J.S." appear just before tear which evidently removed the final initial. MS², dated "5–14–18", is also on the blue-lined, yellowish-brown pad paper (273 × 201.5 mm, 52 mm h. sp.). Corresponding tears and other physical evidence suggest that the MS² sheet originally followed the MS¹ sheet in the same tablet. MS³, on the back of the fourth ring-binder leaf, bears the date "May 14, 1918" at foot to the left and Cotter's signature to the right; "Copy" is written below the signature. The title on MS³ is written "Looking at a Portrait." On the front of the leaf is a copy of "The Goal" [21, MS].

TS¹, on unwatermarked paper (280.5 × 215.5 mm), carries the penciled page number "2" in the upper left corner. On TS¹⁻³, "Looking at a Portrait" appears above typescript of "To ———" [50, TS¹⁻³].

50. TO ———

*MS, holograph, signed; TS¹, "Shadows"-A; TS², "Shadows"-B; TS³, "Shadows"-C; TS⁴, "Shadows"-D; AME 1921

MS Alterations: [*omit first stanza*]] "All the freshness of the dawn | Glories in your shining face, | All the softness of the night | Breathes within each aery grace." *deleted in pencil (Stanza also deleted in pencil on* TS[1], *canceled in black ink on* TS[2-3]. *Word* "aery" *in last line of canceled stanza on* MS *becomes* "airy", TS[1-3]. *Stanza does not appear on* TS[4]+.)

7 heaven . . . smile,] *may be w.o. erasure*

Variants: 2, 4, 6, 8 [*indented three spaces*]] *indented two spaces* AME 1921
2 wrack] wreck TS[4]
6 denied,] ∼ᴧ TS[1-4]
6 cries,] ∼ᴧ TS[1]+
7 smile,] ∼ᴧ TS[1]+

Note: The MS, on the back of the sixth ring-binder leaf, is dated "July 8, 1918." and signed at foot. "Copy" is written beneath Cotter's signature. On the front of the leaf is a copy of "Is It Because I Am Black?" [11, MS]. "To" is followed with "————" only on MS; on TS[1-4] title is "To"; on AME 1921 title is "TO".

On unwatermarked paper (280.5 × 215.5 mm), TS[1] carries the penciled page number "2" in the upper left corner. A curved penciled line on each side of the deleted first stanza of "To ————" on TS[2] marks that stanza for cancellation. "To ————" appears below typescript of "Looking at a Portrait" [49, TS[1-3]] on TS[1-3] and above "Moloch" [51, TS[3]] on TS[4].

51. MOLOCH

MS[1], holograph, initialed; *MS[2], holograph, initialed; TS[1], "Shadows"-A; TS[2], "Shadows"-B; TS[3], "Shadows"-D; AME 1921

Emendation: 2 Flanders'] ∼ᴧ MS[1]; Flander's MS[2]+

MS[1] Alterations: 1 Old] *purplish stain on lower part of* "O"
1 walks] *purplish stain on loop of* "l"
7 anodyne] "e" *appears to have been added later*
12 blazon] *lower part of loop of* "z" *may be traced over in purple ink*
16 shames] *interlined above canceled* "gelds"?

MS[2] Alterations: 1 Old] "ld" *traced over or perhaps written in purple ink*
7 Cries] *pencil line through word appears to be accidental*
9 heart] "h" *w.o. illeg.*
10 holds] "ds" *w.o. illeg.*
13 Moloch] *second* "o" *appears to be w.o. illeg.*

Variants: 2, 4, 6, 8, 10, 12 [*indented three spaces*]] *indented two spaces* AME
   1921
3 Where] When TS[1]+
7 anodyne∧] ∼, MS[1]
8 youths] youth MS[1]
9 tonight] to night MS[1]; to-night TS[1–3]
13–16 Tear . . . men.] *stanza is deleted in pencil on* TS[1], *deleted in black ink on*
   TS[2], *and entirely absent from* TS[3], AME 1921

Note: MS[1], written vertically on the back of white, wove, unwatermarked
envelope (98 × 190.5 mm), is dated "9–27–'18" above initials "J.S.C. Jr."
below the poem. It carries no title. (See illustration.) Front of envelope
bears printed return address "LEVY BROS. | Correct Apparel | for
Men, Youths and Boys | LOUISVILLE, KENTUCKY." It is addressed
to "Jos. S. Cotter, | 2306 Magazine, City." and is postmarked "LOUIS-
VILLE | SEP 26 | 10 AM | 1918 | K.Y." On MS[2], on the front of
the ninth ring-binder leaf, the significance of a penciled check mark just
below the title is uncertain. MS[2] carries the following notations below the
poem: to the left, the date "9–27–'18" above Cotter's initials; to the right,
"Copy." On the back of the leaf is a copy of "Rain Music" [52, MS].
   TS[1], on unwatermarked paper (280 × 215.5 mm), carries the page num-
ber "3" penciled in the upper left corner. A curved, penciled line on each
side of the deleted last stanza of "Moloch" on TS[2] (see variant of lines
13–16, above) marks that stanza for cancellation. On TS[1–2], "Moloch" is
typed at the top of the page above typescript of "Rain Music" [52, TS[1–2]].
"Moloch" is typed below "To ———" [50, TS[4]] on TS[3].

52. RAIN MUSIC

MS, holograph; TS[1], "Shadows"-A; TS[2], "Shadows"-B; AME 1921

MS Alterations: 10 greening] *penciled line below* "een" *is of unclear significance*
14 tatoo —] *dash over erased comma or semicolon*

Variants: 2, 4, 6, 8, 10, 12, 14, 16 [*indented two spaces*]] *marked to indent four*
   spaces TS[1]; *indented three spaces* TS[2]
5, 13 Slender,] ∼∧ TS[1]+
15 God∧] ∼, TS[1]+
15 Musician∧] ∼, TS[1]+

Note: The MS, written on the back of the ninth leaf of the ring binder, bears the notation "Copy this." at foot. Written vertically in black ink in the right margin is a notation in what appears to be the hand of Joseph Seamon Cotter, Sr.: "Joseph S. Cotter Jr.'s last copied poem [*about six blank spaces*] January–1919". Below this note is the signature "Joseph S. Cotter Sr". Following "Sr" in the signature is what appears to be an apostrophe followed by "s"; the significance of this is unclear. The text of the poem itself appears to be in the hand of Cotter Jr. On the front of the manuscript leaf is a copy of "Moloch" [51, MS²].

On unwatermarked paper (280 × 215.5 mm), TS¹ bears the page number "3" penciled in the upper left corner. TS¹⁻² present the text of "Rain Music" below typescript of "Moloch" [51, TS¹⁻²].

53. REWARD

*MS, holograph, signed; TS¹, "Shadows"-A; TS², "Shadows"-B; TS³, "Shadows"-C; AME 1921

MS Alterations: 7 passion of soul] *w.o. erasure*
8 dove] *upper loop of* "d" *partially erased during erasure on line above*

Variants: 2, 4, 6, 8, 10, 12 [*indented two spaces*]] *indented three spaces* TS²⁻³
7 And] and TS¹ (*initial letter inadvertently written in lower case in penciled correction of typographical error which left out* "n")
11 lips,] ~∧ TS¹⁻³

Note: The MS, written on the back of the first leaf of the ring binder, bears the date "April 30, 1918" to the left and Cotter's signature to the right at foot. "Copy" is written below the signature. MS title is written "Reward.", with "r" written over a prior mark, perhaps also "r". On the front of the manuscript leaf is a copy of "Remembrance" [22, MS].

A penciled page number "4" is in the upper left corner of TS¹, which is on unwatermarked paper (280 × 216 mm). An apparent erasure above the title of "Reward" at head of TS¹ is probably erased title typed in error. TS¹⁻³ carry "Reward" on the top half of the page, above typescript of "Why?" [54, TS¹⁻³].

54. WHY?

*MS, holograph, signed; TS¹, "Shadows"-A; TS², "Shadows"-B; TS³, "Shadows"-C; AME 1921

Emendation: 7 smile's] TS¹+; smiles' MS

MS Alterations: 2 does] *final stroke of "s" appears to be traced over in purple ink*
2 she] *parts of "s" and "h" appear to be traced over in purple ink*
4 hail] "ai" *w.o. illeg. letters*

Variants: 2, 4, 6, 8, 10, 12 [*indented one space*]] *marked to indent three spaces* TS¹; *indented three spaces* TS²⁻³; *indented two spaces* AME 1921

Note: Written on the back of the second ring-binder leaf, the MS carries the date "May 5, 1918" and Cotter's signature below the poem. "Copy" is written below the signature. On the front of the manuscript leaf is a text of "On Hearing Helen Hagan Play" [60, MS].

TS¹, on unwatermarked paper (280 × 216 mm), carries the page number "4" in the upper left corner. See Apparatus note to "Reward" [53], above, regarding erasure at top of TS¹. On TS¹⁻³, "Why?" occupies the lower half of the page, below typescript of "Reward" [53, TS¹⁻³]. Title on TS¹⁻³ is "Why", without question mark.

55. SONNET

*MS, holograph, signed; TS¹, "Shadows"-A; TS², "Shadows"-B; TS³, "Shadows"-C; AME 1921

Emendation: 13 grieve] TS¹+; greive MS

MS Alterations: 3 And if their] *w.o. erased words* "And if their"?
8 wind-blown] *appears to be w.o. erasure*
10 affair;] *semicolon w.o. comma?*
12 broken] *w.o. erasure with heavy pressure; penciled check mark below word*
12 spare;] *semicolon w.o. comma?*

Variants: 1 Mighty] mighty TS¹+
2, 3, 6, 7, 10, 12, 14 [*indentation*]] *no indentation* TS¹+
4 sod.] ∼, TS¹+
5 th'] the TS²+

6 Why . . . When,] why . . . when, TS¹⁻³; why . . . when. AME 1921
10 And, smiling,] ∼ₐ ∼ₐ TS¹+
13 rife,] ∼; AME 1921

Note: The MS, written on the back of the seventh leaf of the ring binder, carries the date "July 27, 1918", Cotter's signature, and the notation "Copy" at foot. A period follows the title on the MS. Extensive, thorough erasures on several parts of the MS, often written over, are difficult to locate and specifically note. On the front of the manuscript leaf is a copy of "And What Shall You Say?" [10, MS].

TS¹ is on unwatermarked paper (279.5 × 216 mm) and carries the penciled page number "5" in the upper left corner. "- - - - -Snnet- - - -" is typed at head on the verso of TS¹. On TS¹⁻³, the "Sonnet" appears above typescript of "Love's Demesne" [56, TS¹⁻³].

56. LOVE'S DEMESNE

MS¹, holograph draft, signed; *MS², holograph, initialed; TS¹, "Shadows"-A; TS², "Shadows"-B; TS³, "Shadows"-C; AME 1921

MS¹ Alterations: 3 blue-girt robes of] *w.o. erased words*
†6 Sorrow] "S" *w.o.* "s"
7 My . . . o'er] *w.o. erased words*
†8 To . . . drear] *w.o. erased words*
9 are] *w.o. erasure*
14 the] *w.o. erasure*
†15 purpled-walls] "s" *w.o. illeg.*

MS² Alterations: 5 days when] *w.o. possible erasure*
5 was] "s" *w.o. illeg.*
8 Unto this] *w.o. erasure*
14 serene,] *w.o. possible erasure*
15 On] *w.o. erasure, including erased* "On" *interlined above*
16 demesne] *small penciled check mark below word is of unclear significance*

Variants: [*stanzas not numbered*]] *stanzas numbered* "I", "II", "III", "IV" MS¹
2, 4, 6, 8, 10, 12, 14, 16 [*indented two spaces*]] *marked to indent three spaces* TS¹; *indented three spaces* TS²⁻³
5 hope] Hope MS¹

6 sorrow] Sorrow MS[1]; sorrows AME 1921
8 Unto this] To this drear MS[1]
9 motley] a motley AME 1921
11 aloft] a loft TS[1-3]
12 heart's] hearts' MS[1]
14 serene,] ∼∧ MS[1]
15 On] Of MS[1]
15 purpled∧walls] ∼-∼ MS[1]

Note: The untitled MS[1] draft on blue-ruled, yellowish-brown pad paper (252 × 200 mm, 48.5 mm t. sp.), bears the date "9–27–'18" and Cotter's signature at foot. In the space between the third and fourth stanzas is the canceled beginning of another poem, still partly legible: "Ah [*blank space*] saw light, | Never to the man who never knew life | And [*illeg.*]." These canceled lines are written upside down in relation to the draft of "Love's Demesne." On the reverse side of MS[1] is a copy of the last six lines of Sonnet IV [29, MS[2]] written above a copy of the previously unpublished poem beginning "Never, never shall I clothe" [62, MS]. MS[2], on the back of the eighth ring-binder leaf, is dated "9–27–'18." above Cotter's initials in the lower left corner; "Copy" is written to the right at foot. On the front of the manuscript leaf is a copy of "Is This the Price of Love?" [5, MS].

On unwatermarked paper (279.5 × 216 mm), TS[1] carries the penciled page number "5" in the upper left corner. See Apparatus note to "Sonnet" [55] regarding the typing on the verso of TS[1]. "Love's Demesne" is typed below "Sonnet" [55, TS[1-3]] on TS[1-3].

57. AFRICA

*MS, holograph, initialed; TS[1], "Shadows"-A; TS[2], "Shadows"-B; TS[3], "Shadows"-C; AME 1921

MS Alterations: 9 and] *small penciled check mark below word is of unclear significance*
9 sword,] *comma w.o. possible erasure*
13–14 Sear . . . part.] *lines w.o. erased words*
14+ *three erased lines following line 14 appear to be remnant of superseded draft of* "Africa"

Variants: 2, 3, 6, 7, 10, 12 [*indentation*]] *no indentation* TS[1]+

2 centuries'] centurie's TS^1
6 upward,] $\sim_\wedge$ TS^1+
12 puny,] $\sim_\wedge$ TS^1+

Note: MS, written on the back of the tenth ring-binder leaf, carries the notation "Copy", the date "May 3, 1918" (partially underlined), and Cotter's initials at foot. On the front of the leaf is a copy of "A Prayer" [3, MS].

TS^1, on unwatermarked paper (184.5 irreg. × 215 mm), carries the penciled page number "6" in the upper left corner.

58. THEODORE ROOSEVELT

*MS; TS^1, "Shadows"-A; TS^2, "Shadows"-B; TS^3, "Shadows"-C; AME 1921

Emendations: 2 him.] TS^1+; $\sim_\wedge$ MS
7 again] TS^1+; aga⟨   ⟩ MS (*because of tear, only first three letters of "again" remain*)
9 gleam] TS^1+; gleame MS
10 goal;] TS^1+; goa⟨   ⟩ MS (*because of tear, only first three letters and loop of "l" of "goal;" remain*)
11 hear] TS^1+; heare MS
11 again] TS^1+; a⟨   ⟩ MS (*because of tear, only first letter of "again" remains*)
12 nation's soul.] TS^1+; nation's ⟨   ⟩ MS ("*soul.*" *removed by tear*)
13 fearful moan,] TS^1+; fearful ⟨   ⟩ MS (*everything following first loop of "m" of "moan" obliterated by tear*)

MS Alterations: 1 dust] *w.o. erasure*
1 bore] "o" *w.o. illeg.*
2 ye] *w.o. illeg.*
3 light] "g" *w.o. illeg.*
4 He . . . steps] *w.o. erasure*
4 who] *w.o. illeg.*
7 hear] "r" *w.o. illeg.*
8 right?] *vertical penciled line following* "?" *is of unclear meaning*
11 ye] "e" *written just before and over erasure*
11 redeem] *second* "e" *w.o. illeg.*

13 Rise] *w.o. erasure*

Variants: 2, 4, 6, 8, 10, 12 [*indented two spaces*]] *indented three spaces* TS¹; *no indentation* TS²⁻³
2 maw‸] ∼, TS¹+
8 right] might TS¹+

Note: The MS, on blue-ruled, yellowish-brown pad paper (254 irreg. × 204 irreg. mm, approx. 34 mm h. sp.), has suffered large tears. The title on MS is underlined with three lines of decreasing length. MS appears to be written in the hand of Joseph Seamon Cotter, Sr., which would correspond with the notation typed at foot of TS¹⁻³ (see below). Dated "Jan. 10–1919.", the MS evidently gives the text as dictated by Cotter Jr. and transcribed by Cotter Sr. The "Jr." of the signature on the manuscript is written over and corrected, as if written by someone relatively unaccustomed to writing the abbreviation. The overall appearance of the signature suggests that Cotter Sr. signed his son's name to the poem.

On a torn sheet of unwatermarked onionskin paper (255 irreg. × 204 mm), TS¹ carries the page number "7" penciled in the upper left corner; a "6" may have been penciled and erased to the right above the "7". The following is typed at foot of TS¹⁻³: "Joseph S. Cotter, Jr. ‖ January 10–1919. ‖ The above sonnet was young Cotter's last ‖ poem. He dictated it to his father." An identically worded annotation appears below the text of the poem as printed in the *A.M.E. Zion Quarterly Review* (AME 1921).

Uncollected Poems

59. ODE TO DEMOCRACY

*TS¹, carbon of lost original; TS², carbon of lost original different from TS¹

Emendation: 16 Divine,"] ∼", TS¹⁻²

TS¹ Alterations: 3 deployed thy bark?] "ployed thy bark?" *appears to be typed on the carbon over erasure*
9 the] *preceded by erased* "t"
12 speaks] *second* "s" *typed on wine-colored ribbon over erasure; erasure continues after* "speaks"
13 endless shore,] "less shore," *appears to be typed on the carbon over erasure*

†16 Divine",] *comma handwritten, black ink*
20 Thru] "T" *typed on wine-colored ribbon over erasure*
23 yet] "y" *appears to be typed on the carbon over erased letter*
24 troubled sea] "d sea" *typed on wine-colored ribbon over erasure*
33 strength] "e" *typed on the carbon over* "i"?

Variant: 12 Democracy (*line begins thirteen spaces to left of all other lines*)]
   begins ten spaces to left TS²

Note: TS¹, on a piece of white, wove, PRE-EMINENT watermarked paper
(220 × 161.5 irreg. mm) evidently cut from a standard sheet of typing
paper, bears a large, penciled ex that crosses out the entire text of the
poem. Written vertically in the lower left margin is the notation

> This was 13th poem in Original
> "Band of Gideon"
> By Joseph S. Cotter, Jr.

The notation, in faded black ink, appears to be in the hand of Cotter Sr. See
the Typescripts section of the Textual Commentary on the relationship of
TS¹ to the early "Gideon" typescripts.

TS² is on a sheet of torn, white, wove, unwatermarked onionskin paper
(279 × 215 mm). The right and left margins are marked with what appears
to be a red crayoned line drawn vertically from the top to the bottom of
the page, set in 30 mm from the left edge of the paper and about 18 mm,
very irregularly, from the right edge of the paper. "Joseph S. Cotter, Jr."
is typed at foot, to the right below a row of asterisks. "J.S. Cotter Jr?" is
written diagonally in the upper right corner in black ink in a hand other
than that of Cotter Jr. or Cotter Sr.

60. ON HEARING HELEN HAGAN PLAY

*MS, holograph

MS Alterations: 4 rain,] *the apparent comma crosses last stroke of* "n" *and curves
   to resemble* "s" *added later; thus,* "rains" *is possibly the reading*
7 tossed] *first* "s" *w.o. illeg.*
13 paeans] *first* "a" *w.o. possible* "e"
18 flowed] "w" *w.o. illeg.*
20 softly] "ft" *w.o. illeg.*

Note: The MS, on the front of the second ring-binder leaf, carries a penciled "4." in the upper left margin and two check marks to the right at foot. A period follows the title. In line 4, the handwriting of "bosom" is difficult to decipher, and its reading is not absolutely certain. Line 19 is set in about one space, but the indentation was probably not intentional. On the back of the manuscript leaf is a copy of "Why?" [54, MS].

61. FULL WELL HE KNEW THE GALL OF BROKEN SPIRIT

*MS, holograph, initialed

MS Alteration: 4 crucifixioned] "ci" *w.o. illeg.*

Note: The untitled poem is written vertically to the right across blue-ruled lines on the back of a sheet of yellowish-brown pad paper (272 × 201.5 mm) and is initialed "J.S.C. Jr" at foot. On the front of the leaf is a copy of "Night Winds" [47, MS¹].

62. NEVER, NEVER SHALL I CLOTHE

*MS, holograph

MS Alterations: 2 Fears] "F" *may be w.o. prior letter,* "f"?
5 Fear] "F" *may be w.o. prior* "f"?
7 'tis led] *w.o. erased words*

Note: Written on blue-ruled, yellowish-brown pad paper (252 × 200 mm, 48 mm h. sp.), the poem appears between two large, pencil-drawn braces that bracket all eight lines. MS carries no title. At foot a penciled line extends across the page. This eight-line poem is written below a copy of the last six lines of Sonnet IV [29, MS²]. On the reverse of the manuscript leaf is a copy of "Love's Demesne" [56, MS¹].

63. YOUR HANDS IN MY HANDS

*MS, holograph, initialed

Note: Written on blue-ruled, yellowish-brown pad paper (252.5 × 202 mm, 52 mm h. sp.), MS bears the initials "J.S.C., Jr." at foot. There is no title.

64. MY LYRE IS STRUNG WITH GOLDEN THREADS OF LOVE

*MS, holograph

MS Alterations: 3 My caroling] *w.o. erasure*
4 Full-burthened] *w.o. erasure*
4 spirit's] "t's" *w.o. illeg.*
5 Of] "f" *w.o. illeg.*
7 Sweet] "S" *may be w.o.* "s"
8 cadenced] *w.o. erasure*
8 organed] *w.o. erasure*
8 swell] "e" *w.o. illeg.*
8 roll] *w.o. prior word, probably also* "roll"
9 rythm] "m" *w.o. erasure*
10 skies] "ie" *w.o. erasure*
11 Clearly] *w.o. erasure, apparent comma following probable remnant of erased material*
11 unto] "u" *may be w.o. illeg.*
11 shining] "ing" *w.o. erasure*
12 soft, warm] *w.o. erasure*
13 O] *w.o. erasure*

Note: MS, written on blue-ruled, yellowish-brown pad paper (248 × 204 mm, 26 mm h. sp.), carries a roman "I." at head. This poem is apparently a trial, considered and rejected for first position in the "Out of the Shadows" sonnet sequence [26–44]. Note that the final couplet is identical to the final couplet of the sonnet actually incorporated into the sequence as Sonnet I [26]. In line 2 "Harped" is very faint, its reading not absolutely certain. On the reverse side of the manuscript leaf is a copy of Sonnet II of the sequence [27, MS¹].

65. DOWN FROM THE GOLDEN STRINGS OF MY HEART'S LYRE

*MS, holograph, initialed

MS Alterations: 5 harmony] "y" *w.o. erased* "ies"?
7 devotee,] *apparent erased punctuation mark between* "devotee" *and comma*
11 unto] "un" *w.o. illeg.*

Note: Written on the back of the first school-tablet leaf, MS carries a roman

"I" at head. The entire text of the sonnet is canceled with a large pen-
ciled ex and wavy lines. The dates "8–13–'18" and "10–1–'18" and Cotter
Jr.'s initials are on successive lines in the lower left corner. Just below the
text of the poem, "Omit" is written, twice underlined. On the front of the
manuscript leaf is a copy of Sonnet II [27, MS^2].

This sonnet appears to be a second trial (see Apparatus note to poem
64), rejected as the first sonnet of the "Out of the Shadows" sequence [26–
44]. As in unpublished poem number 64, the final couplet of poem number
65 is identical to that of the sonnet finally incorporated into the sequence
as Sonnet I [26]. Note, too, that lines 8, 11, and 12 are virtually the same
for poems 64 and 65.

Notes

Joseph Seamon Cotter, Jr.: Toward
a Reconsideration

1. Information in this paragraph was derived from Joseph Seamon Cotter, Sr.'s memoir "Joseph S. Cotter, Jr.," ts., Cotter Papers, Western Branch, Louisville Free Public Library, Louisville, n. pag.; and Ann Allen Shockley, "Joseph S. Cotter, Sr.: Biographical Sketch of a Black Louisville Bard," *CLA Journal* 18 (1975): 331–37 *et passim*. The Cotter Sr. memoir was published in part in somewhat altered form in *Caroling Dusk: An Anthology of Verse by Negro Poets*, ed. Countee Cullen (New York: Harper, 1927) 99–100.

   Material within quotation marks is from chapter 5 of Joseph Seamon Cotter, Sr.'s untitled, unpublished autobiography, ts., Cotter Papers, n. pag., as quoted by Shockley 331. The birthdate of Cotter Jr. is recorded on his baptismal certificate from Our Merciful Saviour Episcopal Church, Louisville, which is filed with the Cotter Papers. All citations to the Cotter Papers throughout these notes refer to the collection of Cotter family papers housed in the Western Branch of the Louisville Free Public Library, Louisville, Kentucky.

2. Shockley 331–32. For a recent biographical sketch of the senior Cotter and a discussion of his major publications, see A. Russell Brooks, "Joseph Seamon Cotter, Sr.," in *Afro-American Writers before the Harlem Renaissance*, ed. Trudier Harris and Thadious M. Davis, *Dictionary of Literary Biography* 50 (Detroit: Gale, 1986) 62–70.

3. Shockley 332; Brooks 65; Cotter Sr., "Joseph S. Cotter, Jr.," Cotter Papers, n. pag. The quotation is from Cotter Sr.'s memoir.

4. Cotter Sr., "Joseph S. Cotter, Jr.," Cotter Papers, n. pag.

5. Information in this paragraph was derived from Cotter Sr., "Joseph S. Cotter, Jr.," Cotter Papers, n. pag. School reports for Cotter Jr. from both the Western School and the Central Colored High School are filed with the Cotter Papers.

6. Cotter Sr., "Joseph S. Cotter, Jr.," Cotter Papers, n. pag.

7. *Catalog of the Officers, Students and Alumni of Fisk University*, 2nd ed. (Nashville, 1911–12) 69; *Catalog of the Officers and Students of Fisk University* (Nashville, 1912–13) 68. "Staff," *Fisk Herald* December 1912: 6; February 1913: 4; March

1913: 4; April 1913: 6; May 1913: 6; June 1913: 8. Although Cotter left Fisk due to illness before the end of his sophomore year (1912–13), he continued to be listed with the staff of the *Herald* through the June 1913 issue.

8. Cotter Sr., "Joseph S. Cotter, Jr.," Cotter Papers, n. pag.

9. L. H. Hammond, *In the Vanguard of a Race* (New York: Council of Women for Home Missions and Missionary Education Movement of the United States and Canada, 1922) 169. Cotter is listed as "City Editor" on the masthead of the November 10, 1917, issue of the *Louisville Leader*, p. 2. The November 10, 1917, issue is only the second issue of the weekly *Leader*. For the period of Cotter's life, it is the only issue available at the Kentucky Library, Western Kentucky University, Bowling Green, where the most complete file of the *Leader* is held on microfilm.

10. The quotation is taken from a clipping of a newspaper article entitled "Vale Segregation"; the article concludes with the initials "J.S.C., Jr." "The Louisville Leader" is written in what appears to be Cotter Jr.'s hand in the left margin, and the date "Nov - 10 - 1917" is handwritten to the right above the article. Cotter handwrote several revisions on the copy of this article filed with the Cotter Papers, including capitalizing the initial letters of the first words of the phrases "Children of the Shadows" and " 'This day is for them.' " All the newspaper clippings referred to in this essay are filed with the Cotter Papers. I have verified the place and date of the "Vale Segregation" piece in the *Louisville Leader*, November 10, 1917, p. 2. To date, I have been unable to verify the place and date of the other cited clippings.

11. Typescripts of the projected work "Out of the Shadows" are discussed in the Textual Commentary and Apparatus.

12. Quoted language is from an undated clipping of a newspaper article entitled "Why We Should Fight for Our Rights"; the article ends with the initials "J.S.C., Jr."

13. The publication date of *The Band of Gideon* was confirmed at the United States Copyright Office, Library of Congress, Washington, D.C.

14. Hammond 169–70.

15. *Crisis* 16 (1918): 64.

16. Cale Young Rice, introduction, *The Band of Gideon and Other Lyrics* (Boston: Cornhill Co., 1918) ix–x. See Ellen Williams, *Harriet Monroe and the Poetry Renaissance: The First Ten Years of Poetry, 1912–22* (Urbana: U of Illinois P, 1977) 22, 65, 70, regarding Rice's association with Monroe and *Poetry*.

17. See the Apparatus notes for manuscript dates of post-*Gideon* poems; see Typescripts section of the Textual Commentary for a discussion of evidence of a projected second book. The three typescripts of Cotter's sonnet "Theodore Roosevelt" carry the following notation typed below the text of the poem: "The above sonnet was young Cotter's last poem. He dictated it to his father." These typescripts, filed with the Cotter Papers, bear the date "January 10 - 1919." See also the Apparatus note to the text of "Theodore Roosevelt" [58].

18. Cotter Sr., "Joseph S. Cotter, Jr.," Cotter Papers, n. pag.

19. Cotter Sr.'s interest in the posthumous publication of his son's poetry is re-
flected in his letter to Arthur B. Spingarn of New York City dated February 2,
1925:

> I send you, under another cover, two magazines that contain all my
> son's poems save "The Band of Gideon."
> I would like to publish all his poems under one cover, but I am too poor
> to do so.

The "magazines" referred to must be the third quarter 1920 and second quarter
1921 issues of the *A.M.E. Zion Quarterly Review* which carried Cotter Jr.'s poems
in "The Poetic Section." In addition to sending copies to Spingarn, Cotter Sr.
sent copies of both issues to Arthur A. Schomburg. Both of Schomburg's copies
are inscribed "To Mr. A.A. Schomburg, August 18 - 1925: | Compliments of
Joseph S. Cotter." The quoted letter from Cotter Sr. to Arthur B. Spingarn
is filed in Folder 8, Box 1, Collection 8, Manuscript Department, Moorland-
Spingarn Research Center, Howard University, Washington, D.C. Arthur A.
Schomburg's copies of the third quarter 1920 and second quarter 1921 issues of
the *A.M.E. Zion Quarterly Review* are at the Schomburg Center for Research in
Black Culture, New York City.

20. An exception is "Rain Music" [52], of the second quarter 1921 *Zion Quarterly*
group, which has appeared in a number of anthologies beginning with James
Weldon Johnson's *The Book of American Negro Poetry* (New York: Harcourt,
1922). In at least one of these anthologies, Newman Ivey White and Walter
Clinton Jackson, eds., *An Anthology of Verse by American Negroes* (1924; Dur-
ham, NC: Moore Publishing Co., 1968), "Rain Music" is ascribed in error
to *The Band of Gideon*, and no anthology that I have seen acknowledges the
poem's original appearance in *Zion Quarterly*. The probable explanation for the
anomaly is that after his son's death Cotter Sr. circulated "Rain Music" for pub-
lication independent of its original placement as part of the final series; some
editors and scholars evidently began to assume the poem was from *Gideon*.

21. One of the plays, "On the Fields of France," a one-act drama of a black Ameri-
can officer and a white officer who die together on a Great War battlefield, was
published in *Crisis* 20 (1920): 77.

22. James Weldon Johnson, ed., *The Book of American Negro Poetry*, rev. ed. (New
York: Harcourt, 1931) 185; Eugene B. Redmond, *Drumvoices: The Mission of
Afro-American Poetry, A Critical History* (Garden City, NY: Anchor-Doubleday,
1976) 168.

23. See discussion of early "Gideon" typescript compilation in the Typescripts
section of the Textual Commentary.

24. Cotter's biblical source is Judges 6–8. In my brief introductory article, "Joseph
Seamon Cotter, Jr.," in *Afro-American Writers before the Harlem Renaissance*, ed.
Trudier Harris and Thadious M. Davis, *Dictionary of Literary Biography* 50 (De-
troit: Gale, 1986) 70–73, there is a preliminary version of the approach to "The
Band of Gideon" offered here.

25. Robert T. Kerlin, *Negro Poets and Their Poems*, 3rd ed. (Washington, DC: Associated, 1935) 83. See Hammond 172 for remarks in a similar vein.

26. Judges 8.4–9.

27. For a solid historical account, see Arthur E. Barbeau and Florette Henri, *The Unknown Soldiers: Black American Troops in World War I* (Philadelphia: Temple UP, 1974).

28. Cotter Sr., "Joseph S. Cotter, Jr.," Cotter Papers, n. pag. Clippings of Cotter's newspaper articles on issues related to the war are on file at Western Branch, Louisville Free Public Library.

29. Paul Fussell, *The Great War and Modern Memory* (New York: Oxford UP, 1975) 174.

30. See James Weldon Johnson, "Views and Reviews," *New York Age* 12 July 1917: 4; and *Crisis* 15 (1918): 270.

31. Combining as it does technical features of both the Italian and English sonnet forms, "Sonnet to Negro Soldiers" is not as formally traditional as it may seem on first reading.

32. W. E. B. Du Bois, unsigned editorial, "The Black Soldier," *Crisis* 16 (1918): 60; "Sonnet to Negro Soldiers" is on page 64 of the same issue.

33. "To the White Fiends," *Liberator* 2 (Sept. 1919): 25; "A Roman Holiday" and "If We Must Die," *Liberator* 2 (July 1919): 21. Cited in Wayne F. Cooper, ed., *The Passion of Claude McKay: Selected Poetry and Prose, 1912–1948* (New York: Schocken, 1973) 123–24.

34. Du Bois, unsigned editorial, "The Black Soldier" 60. In a newspaper article entitled "After the War, Then What?" Cotter surveys post–Great War world prospects, expressing views similar to those taken by Du Bois in this *Crisis* editorial. For post-war America, Cotter foresees "the Negro invested with practically all his civil rights." The article, concluding with the initials "J.S.C., Jr.," is on an unidentified newspaper clipping filed with the Cotter Papers.

35. See Apparatus notes on individual texts of "The Mulatto to His Critics" [2] regarding evidence that "The Mulatto" was probably in first position in an early, prepublication arrangement of the "Gideon" poems.

36. Chesnutt's views on a "future American race" may be found in his articles "The Future American: What the Race Is Likely to Become in the Process of Time," *Boston Evening Transcript* 18 Aug. 1900: 20; "The Future American: A Stream of Dark Blood in the Veins of the Southern Whites," *Boston Evening Transcript* 25 Aug. 1900: 15; "The Future American: A Complete Race — Amalgamation Likely to Occur," *Boston Evening Transcript* 1 Sept. 1900: 24.

37. Cotter conveyed the new, more assertive post-war mood in newspaper articles entitled "Why We Should Fight for Our Rights," "After the War, Then What?," and "A Step in the Right Direction," which are filed with the Cotter Papers. "A Step in the Right Direction" is annotated "Nov. 2 - 1917" and "Lou. Leader" in what appears to be Cotter Jr.'s hand; no date or name of newspaper appears on the other two articles. Each article ends with the typeset initials "J.S.C., Jr."

38. Johnson, ed. *The Book of American Negro Poetry*, rev. ed., 140.
39. Both "Tired" and "The Scarlet Woman" are in Johnson, ed., *The Book of American Negro Poetry*, rev. ed., 144–46.
40. Johnson, ed., *The Book of American Negro Poetry*, rev. ed., 185.
41. The dedication reads, "IN MEMORY | OF | MY SISTER | FLORENCE OLIVIA COTTER".
42. A helpful though necessarily incomplete listing of anthology appearances of Cotter's poems is given in Jessamine S. Kallenbach, comp., *Index to Black American Literary Anthologies* (Boston: Hall, 1979) 21. In 1969 the McGrath Publishing Co., College Park, MD, reprinted the original 1918 Cornhill edition of *The Band of Gideon*.
43. See note 20 above.
44. Dates on individual sonnet series manuscripts range from August 13 to November 21, 1918. See Apparatus notes to texts of the sonnets.
45. See Apparatus notes to texts of uncollected poems numbered 64 and 65.
46. Regarding dating, see Apparatus note to Sonnet V [30]. Indicative of the state of Cotter's illness about this time is a letter dated October 24, 1918, which he received from a hospital supply company (see Apparatus note to Sonnet XV [40, MS¹]).
47. References to Taylor's "The Preface," *The Poems of Edward Taylor*, ed. Donald E. Stanford (New Haven: Yale UP, 1960) 387–88, and to Johnson's "The Creation," *God's Trombones: Seven Negro Sermons in Verse* (New York: Viking, 1927) 17–20, are not meant to suggest direct influence but simply to point to a tradition that Cotter appears to draw upon. Taylor's seventeenth-century New England poems were discovered and published in the late 1930s, and of course *God's Trombones*, too, was published after Cotter's death.
48. The baptismal certificate is filed with the Cotter Papers.
49. The evolution of this memorable line from early draft form to fair copy is traceable in Cotter's manuscripts; see Apparatus on Sonnet XIX [44].
50. See Apparatus note to "Is It Because I Am Black?" [11] for documentation of how an editor, perhaps Jessie Fauset, requested that Cotter give a more positive turn to "Is It Because I Am Black?" by adding thematically contrastive stanzas: "in spite of being black."
51. For a recent, concise discussion of sonnet forms, see Miller Williams, *Patterns of Poetry: An Encyclopedia of Forms* (Baton Rouge: Louisiana State UP, 1986) 80–83.
52. See Apparatus note on texts of "Theodore Roosevelt" [58].
53. "Theodore Roosevelt," *Crisis* 17 (1919): 163. The editorial is unsigned, and authorship is uncertain as Du Bois was in Europe at the time; but in any case it was produced under Du Bois's general editorship.
54. See Apparatus note on texts of "Theodore Roosevelt" [58].
55. See editorial sections headed "Africa," "Reconstruction and Africa," and "Not 'Separatism,'" and the NAACP report "Africa and the World Democracy," *Crisis* 17 (1919): 164–66, 173–76. The phrase "redemption of Africa" appears in

the section headed "Not 'Separatism,'" p. 166. It is virtually certain that this editorial material, though unsigned, is by Du Bois. The NAACP report was evidently prepared by John R. Shillady, NAACP Secretary.

56. Du Bois's allusion to his work on the Pan-African Conference appears in the second letter, dated at "Paris, December 14, 1918.", of two letters comprising the editorial section headed "Letters from Dr. Du Bois," *Crisis* 17 (1919): 164.

Textual Commentary

1. In her article "Jessie Redmon Fauset," in *Afro-American Writers from the Harlem Renaissance to 1940*, ed. Trudier Harris and Thadious M. Davis, *Dictionary of Literary Biography* 51 (Detroit: Gale, 1987) 76–86, Carolyn Wedin Sylvander notes, "From 1918 to 1919 Fauset completed a Master of Arts degree at the University of Pennsylvania and was, by this time, working with W. E. B. Du Bois and the *Crisis*. In 1919 she moved to New York as literary editor of that publication . . ." (77).

2. An exception is poem number 13, whose title appears as follows in the early "Gideon" set: "S o n n e t. | TO NEGRO   SOLDIERS." "TO NEGRO SOLDIERS." is underlined.

3. Suggestive of the revision process is the fact that early "Gideon" poems that are crossed out appear without exception in later "Gideon," often in revised form. Early "Gideon" poems that are not crossed out do not appear in later "Gideon."

4. Exceptions are the later "Gideon" typescripts of poem number 8, titled "Then I Would Love You."

5. For example, titles of poems on "Shadows"-A, -B, -C, and -D are typically typed with only initial letters of words capitalized and, often, with hyphens typed before and after: "- - -Reward- - -", "- -To- -". An exception is poem number 58, whose title, "Theodore Roosevelt", is underlined on the "Shadows"-A, -B, and -C sets. Sonnet numbers of the "Out of the Shadows" sonnet sequence are penciled in on "Shadows"-A; on "Shadows"-B and -C they are typed with hyphens: "-1-", "-19-".

6. As noted in the Apparatus, the manuscript of Sonnet XVI [41] is on the back of the leaf carrying the manuscript of Sonnet I [26], another of the three sonnets absent from the Louisville school tablet. Dates on manuscripts of Sonnets II–XII, XIV–XVII [27–37, 39–42] suggest that they were composed in chronological order in the sequence as ultimately presented in the "Shadows"-A, -B, and -C typescripts and in the *Zion Quarterly*. The specific dates, ranging between August 13 and November 21, 1918, appear in the Apparatus notes to the texts of the Sonnets [26–44]. (No dated manuscripts are available for Sonnets I [26], XIII [38], XVIII [43], or XIX [44].) Cotter tended to retain the dates of early drafts when he dated later copies of poems, and one gains the impression that dates on manuscripts almost always reflect original composition dates. The fact that Sonnet XVI was dated and presumably composed in the chronological

sequence reflected in the eventual published version of the sonnets does not, of course, preclude the possibility that it was temporarily withheld from placement in its ultimate position in the sequence during final deliberations by the poet.

7. The cover of this issue gives its volume number in roman numerals as XXXII, while the title page gives the number as XXXI. Since both the cover and the title page of the second quarter, 1921, issue of the journal give its volume number as XXXII, it seems reasonable to assume that the cover of the earlier issue bears a typographical error.

Apr 1990

1- 2/08

1-4/91